W9-BUE-242

Man and God
in the City

266
MIL

FIRST BAPTIST CHURCH LIBRARY
16TH & "O" STS., N.W.
WASHINGTON, D.C. 20036

Kenneth D. Miller | # Man and God in the City

FRIENDSHIP PRESS   NEW YORK

Library of Congress Catalog Card Number: 54-6890

COPYRIGHT, 1954, BY FRIENDSHIP PRESS, INC.

PRINTED IN THE UNITED STATES OF AMERICA

CONTENTS

part one | Man in the City

one | THE DRIVE TO GET AHEAD   1
Why People Live in the City, 2
Climbing up the Ladder, 4
Dangers in Getting Ahead, 6
Getting Ahead and the Christian Ideal, 8
How to Get Ahead as Christians, 10
The City's Missionary Task, 18

two | THE LONELINESS OF CITY
PEOPLE   20
Alone in the Big City, 21
Strangers and Foreigners, 23
Who Are "Our Kind of People"?, 26
Churches That Make Friends, 28

v

CONTENTS

three   THE CITIES AND PEOPLE
ON THE MOVE   34

America on the Move, 35
Our New Defense Communities, 38
Fast Action Called For, 40
Other New Communities, 41
What Moving Does to People, 42
What Moving Does to Churches, 43
Negro and Spanish-speaking Migrants, 44
"Shooting on the Wing", 46

four   SUPERFICIAL URBANITY   48

Externalism, 51
Beneath the Surface, 53
The Churches—The Outside or the
Inside of the Cup?, 54
Within the Cup, 58

five   THE TENSIONS OF CITY LIFE   59

An Anxiety-ridden Age, 60
Personality Problems in the City, 61
Today's Tensions, 62
Spiritual Therapy Needed, 64
Parishioners Can Help, 65
Church Clinics, 66
The Pastoral Ministry, 67

six   THE SOCIAL PROBLEMS OF
THE CITY   70

The Major Problems, 72
Assets and Liabilities in City
Districts, 73

CONTENTS

Burdens Common to All, 76
The Special Burdens of the Poor, 76
Churches as Burden Lifters, 77
Rallying behind Front Line Churches, 78

part two | God in the City

seven | CITIES OF WISTFUL PAGANS   83
Our Mission to Those Outside, 84
Who Are the Unchurched?, 87
The Intellectuals, 87
Labor, 88
The Depressed Groups, 88
Passive Pagans, 89
How Fares Protestantism in America?, 89
Wistful Pagans, 91
Needed: An Aggressive Outreach, 92
Needed: More Friendliness, 94
Needed: Intellectual Alertness, 94
*Needed: A Program at Grips
with Life*, 95
"Don't Fence Me In", 96

eight | THE CHURCH IN THE INNER
CITY   98
What Is the "Inner City"?, 99
Centers of Human Need, 101
The Church and the Inner City, 101
Essentials of a Missionary Program, 103

vii

CONTENTS

nine | THE CHURCH IN THE CITY'S
RESIDENTIAL AREAS 118

The Varied Backgrounds of Cities, 119
Stable Residential Areas, 121
Churches in Residential Areas, 122
Too Many and Too Small, 123
Parochialism, 125
An Outreach Vital, 128
Be Prepared for a Change, 129
Apartment Dwellers, 130
Removal of Members, 131
Changes in the Community, 131

ten | THE CHURCH IN THE SUBURBS 134

Suburban Growth, 134
Why People Move to the Suburbs, 135
Varieties of Suburbs, 135
Their Liabilities, 136
Their Assets, 136
Older Residential Suburbs, 137
New Communities, 138
Industrial Suburbs, 141
The Suburban Church, 142
The Program of the Suburban Church, 145
The Church in the Industrial Suburbs, 147

eleven | GOD AND THE CHURCH
MEMBER 149

Search Your Own Heart, 150
How Does God Speak to Me?, 150

CONTENTS

How Am I to Answer?, 151
Study Your Community, 151
Appraise the Ministry of Your
Church, 152
Tapping Denominational Resources, 152
The Concern of National Home
Mission Boards, 154
Interdenominational Aspects of City
Church Work, 157
Interdenominational Cooperation
on National Level, 161
Conclusions, 162

twelve   GOD IN THE LIFE OF THE
CITY   164
Evidences of God in City Life, 165
The Beauty of the City, 166
God Speaks to Us through
City People, 168
Through Devotees to Good Causes, 168
Self-giving Service, 170
God Speaks in and through Our
Churches, 172
A First-hand Religious Experience, 174

READING LIST   176

All Bible quotations used in this book are from the Revised Standard Version. Copyright, 1946 and 1952, by the Division of Christian Education of the National Council of the Churches of Christ in the United States of America.

ACKNOWLEDGEMENTS

IT IS impossible for me to name all of the individuals whose advice and help have been indispensable to the preparation of this book. Countless friends and colleagues in city church work across the country furnished me with invaluable material dealing with their problems and accomplishments. My fellow workers in the New York City Mission, all unwittingly, provided much of the inspiration for the book and not a few illustrations of outstanding work in this field. Dr. Leslie C. Sayre and the members of the Department of Adult Work of the Joint Commission on Missionary Education of the National Council of Churches have given very valuable criticisms and suggestions.

I am painfully aware of the inadequacy of this treatment of a subject that has been sadly neglected by our Protestant church leaders. My friends who are rendering such outstanding service in the field of research and survey in the city church field will know how inadequate it is on the technical side. But the book is not intended to be technical. Its main purpose is to impress upon our church people the fact that the American city is one of our truly great missionary fields, full of problems, yes, but full, too, of challenges and opportunities.

To my secretary, Miss Hazel L. Bedell, I owe an immeasurable debt of gratitude for the typing and revision of the manuscript.

K. D. M.

part one | MAN IN THE CITY

one | THE DRIVE TO GET AHEAD

"What does it profit a man, to gain the whole world . . ."

I HAVE a friend who finds that each summer he is frequently called down from his summer home in Maine to attend to some urgent affair of business in New York. He tells me that as he leaves behind the lake, the woods, and the mountains and plunges from Grand Central Station down into the fetid subway to be pushed around by a milling crowd of sweating and hurrying individuals, he mutters to himself "Why does anyone want to live and work in this hellhole?"

How many visitors to our American cities remark upon leaving, "This is a nice place to visit, but I wouldn't want to live here. God forbid!"

And yet millions of our fellow Americans, almost two-thirds of them (64 per cent) live in urban areas. And while they may grumble about city life, yearn with nostalgia for the old farm, and make it a point to get as far out of the city

1

over the week ends as the car will take them, most of them really like the city and will not be dragged away from it until retirement age compels it. And all the while more and more people are streaming from town and country and from overseas to swell the number of our city dwellers.

. . .   *Why People Live in the City*

Why do they come? And why do they stay? What does the city offer to them, and what does the city do to these transplanted people of rural and small town backgrounds and to native city dwellers?

There are many answers to be given to these questions, but the determining factor in this pronounced trend to the cities is that people move to the cities propelled by the desire to fulfill "the American ideal of getting ahead." And people stay in the cities because they find it possible there to get ahead in a way and to a degree that is impossible in the country and small towns with their limited opportunities.

Most folks interpret this getting ahead in frankly materialistic terms. People come to the city to get a job or a better job with more opportunity for advancement. But people also come to the city and stay there because the city offers unparalleled opportunities to think creatively, to attain deep insights into human problems, and to make decisions that shape human destiny and determine the pattern of life for a nation and a world.

To be sure, this drive to get ahead is characteristic of all American life. We have never accepted the old world dictum: "Once a peasant always a peasant." This is the characteristic that has made American life so dynamic. It is the factor that has brought to our shores immigrants by the millions from all the nations of the globe. Our immigrants cannot be called "the scum of the earth." Scum represents stagnancy. It never moves. Our immigrants have been people who wanted to get ahead. And so from Ireland, Scotland, Germany, the Scandinavian countries, from southern and eastern Europe and latterly from Mexico and Puerto Rico, for the most part from country villages, millions of people have flooded into American cities to find new opportunities and new freedom. The Negroes are moving from the South to our Northern cities and industrial centers not because they have the wanderlust but because they, too, want to get ahead.

A villager in Maine, finding employment there limited by the exhaustion of the forests and the consequent shutting down of lumber mills, moves to the nearest city to find a steady job and a better chance for his children.

A sharecropper in the South, his meager living imperiled by the introduction of large scale "farm factories," hies himself to the nearest city for employment in mill or factory.

A Southern mountaineer hears that there is a demand for labor in the automobile factories of Detroit and so picks up his family and moves bag and baggage to the Northern city.

Young people with an ambition for a career in music, in art, or on the stage find that they must move to the city to secure the proper training and to have an opportunity to carve out a career.

College trained engineers, physicians, lawyers, and young

3

men and women with a bent for business gravitate to the city, for it is here that they can get ahead most quickly.

. . .   *Climbing up the Ladder*

Immigrant parents scrimp and save so that their children can get an education and move up out of the unskilled labor group into the white collar class.

Negro boys see a Joe Louis, a Sugar Ray Robinson, or a Jackie Robinson driving smart cars and having their names in the headlines, and they, too, harbor secret longings to grow up to be "big shots." Or, on a higher level, they hear of the increasing number of men and women of their race who are making a real contribution to contemporary life as scientists, doctors, lawyers, business men, and government officials and yearn to emulate their example.

Other city youngsters see gangsters moving up into positions of power and prestige, and so they set up their own gangs and follow the pattern of predatory behavior that they have seen work out so "successfully."

In one small New England city an exhaustive social survey was made of all the inhabitants. Each one was pigeonholed as belonging to one or another of these classes: lower-lower, middle-lower, upper-lower; lower-middle, middle-middle, and upper-middle; and lower-upper, middle-upper and upper-upper. Readers of J. P. Marquand's novel *Point of No Return* will recall how he lampoons this doctrinaire classification. They will recall, too, that one of the basic conflicts of the story revolved about the fact that a young man from the upper-middle class tried unsuccessfully

4

to marry a girl from the upper-upper ranges. The fact is that while class lines of this nature are characteristic of American cities, Americans never like to feel themselves shut in by them, and so some of the great sagas of American life are told in terms of "from log cabin to president" or "from office boy to chief executive."

The careers of members of President Eisenhower's cabinet and other appointees illustrate how this American dream of getting ahead is realized.

John Foster Dulles, secretary of state, was the son of a Presbyterian minister in Watertown, New York.

Charles E. Wilson, secretary of defense, was born at Minerva, Ohio, where his parents were schoolteachers.

Herbert Brownell, Jr., attorney general, was born at Peru, Nebraska, where his father was a teacher.

George M. Humphrey, secretary of the treasury, was born at Cheboygan, Michigan, the son of a lawyer there.

Douglas McKay, secretary of the interior, was born at Portland, Oregon, where his father was a carpenter. In his youth he delivered papers, drove a butcher wagon, and ran a small laundry.

Ezra Taft Benson, secretary of agriculture, was born on a farm at Whitney, Idaho.

Sherman Adams, assistant to the president, was born at East Dover, Vermont, where his father ran a grocery store.

Harold E. Stassen, mutual security director, was born at West St. Paul, Minnesota, where his father ran a truck farm. He grew up on the farm, worked in a grocery store and was a bakery pan greaser and a Pullman car conductor in working his way through college.

Out of such backgrounds came these men to the capital city of the country to positions of unusual power and prestige.

. . .   *Dangers in Getting Ahead*

This drive to get ahead is natural and basically healthy. But it is a drive that is easily perverted, and nowhere more readily or with greater accompanying fanfare than in the city. Readers will remember how the hero in *Point of No Return*, in order to realize his ambition to become vice-president of the bank, is careful to conform to the stereotyped mode of living expected of a rising young executive. He moves to the right suburb, associates with the right people, joins the right church. He buys a Buick and dreams of the day when he will ride in a Cadillac behind a liveried chauffeur. Success is measured wholly in material terms and achieved by material means.

Some corporations are going as far as to indicate to their promising young executives what sort of wives they should select and how these wives should behave. They should be college girls but not intellectuals. If they read *The Atlantic Monthly*, they should slip it underneath a slick magazine when company comes. They should realize that their husbands belong to the corporation. "We want men who eat and sleep the company. If a man's first interest is his wife and family, more power to him, but we don't want him." In short, get ahead, get wives who will help you get ahead, no matter what happens to your intellectual life and your family life.

6

A fabulous tycoon of one of our great cities rose from nowhere to head a corporation with assets of over twenty million dollars. He tears through life, always in reach of a telephone. He has three telephones on his desk, three extensions at home, and one in his Chrysler sedan. He is known as the fastest man in town. He is quoted as saying, "Some men run because of ego, some because of avarice, some because of love, but the man who runs because he is frightened runs the fastest. I am afraid of the degradation that a lack of money can bring. In our system the fast and efficient survive, the others perish. I want to survive."

Most city men would regard this as an example of spectacular success. Why not? He has position, power, prestige, and a fortune.

The drive to get ahead operates similarly on all levels of urban society. A child of immigrant parents writes in reminiscence of his public school days: "It was never learning that I associated with that school; only the necessity to succeed, to get ahead of the others in the daily struggle to 'make a good impression' on the teachers. . . . I was the first American child [of my parents]. . . . I was to be the monument of their liberation from the shame of being what they are." [1]

"Work hard, live thriftily, save your money, and some day you will have a home of your own, a car, a television set, and a washing machine, and the American dream will come true for you." This is the city's working philosophy.

So the Irish moved out of the shanties and the tenements

[1] A *Walker in the City*, by Alfred Kazin, pp. 17 ff. New York, Harcourt, Brace and Co., 1951. Used by permission.

up into the police force and the contracting business, to become prominent politicians and papal knights. So the Poles and the Italians moved out of the ditches they dug, left behind their hods of bricks, to enter the professions, the arts, and politics. Many of the Negroes of our cities, even with all the extra restrictions thrown about them, move up the social and economic scale to positions of comparative affluence and influence. They move out of their "ghettoes" when they can, and many are doing so. Where this is not possible, they still strive to move onward and upward within the limitations of the restrictions placed upon them. For they, of all our city people, have the greatest right to dream of getting ahead to escape society's organized effort to "keep them in their place."

. . . *Getting Ahead and the Christian Ideal*

So city people all want to get ahead. That is why they are there. That is what makes a city tick. It accounts for the city's high strung disposition and for its magnificent achievements. And what is wrong with the drive to get ahead? Surely there is no virtue in standing still and accepting for oneself the status quo. But we as Christians do need to look at this all pervading dynamism in the light of the principles and standards of the gospel of Christ we are here to proclaim. And it is then that doubts intrude.

I recall Halford Luccock saying that most people's idea of evolution is the ascent from the nasty amoeba to Uncle Frederick standing radiant, clothed in a Prince Albert, at the top of a long spiral slope, one hand resting on the First

8

National Bank, the other on the First Presbyterian Church.

But remember the words of Jesus: "Whoever would be first among you must be your slave"; "Everyone who exalts himself will be humbled"; "A man's life does not consist in the abundance of his possessions"; "What will it profit a man, if he gains the whole world and forfeits his life?"

The city man is in danger of losing his soul in the drive to get ahead. To save the soul of man and to give the city a soul is the task of the churches.

Modern theology is rightly stressing the centrality of the Cross and the Resurrection. But one reason Christ came to the Cross was because he took such sharp issue with the prevailing philosophy of his day. And the Resurrected Lord lives on as one who stands for such values as the sacredness of the human personality, faith in man, the responsibility of society to provide opportunities for the abundant life, the reality of human fellowship, the solidarity of mankind, love as the motive of life, and the subordination of private gain to the public welfare in the spirit of service.

If our churches are to save the souls of city men and produce a climate favorable to spiritual values, their gospel must embody these truths. We need boldly and unequivocally to declare that civilization is to be judged by its human balance sheet, by what happens to human beings in the economic process, not by the things produced. Moreover, these values must be embodied in the preaching and in the program of our city churches. The churches should demonstrate the truth they proclaim, taking the often unpracticed truths of the gospel and making them walk the city streets again.

Yet this aspect of the gospel is all too often muted. We find city churches, church organizations and leaders surrendering to a materialistic philosophy of getting ahead. Churches measure themselves and are measured by their size, the multiplicity of their activities, and the amount of their budget, rather than by their impact upon individuals and the community. Public relations experts take hold of the churches on the theory that their job is "to sell Jesus Christ to the public." Publicity at any price and a favorable impression upon the wealthy is a *sine qua non*. Ministers patronize clipping bureaus. We want the church to achieve prestige, power, and possessions. Then we wonder why the church is lost in city life. It is too busy saying "me, too" to the prevailing philosophy of city people.

Christ surely would be interested in having people get ahead so as to provide the economic base for a good life. But he would want *all* people to get ahead to that point, not simply the favored few, the ruthless few, and the fast and efficient few. Then he would want all to understand that the economic base is only the base and that upon it must be built the structure of our real life, in which goodness, self-sacrificing love, and responsibility for meeting human needs are much more important than accumulating goods.

... *How to Get Ahead as Christians*

Churches of all kinds are working at this essential missionary task of placing before city people the Christian gospel and helping them to get ahead in the realization of the ideals and standards embodied therein.

10

Some years ago the leaders of the women's interdenominational missionary program in one of our cities were gathered to make their plans for the year. Strangely enough, it soon became obvious that some of the leaders were thinking of missions solely in terms of a charitable effort on behalf of people far removed from them—an effort that was to be fully expressed by gifts to the missionary budgets of the denominational boards. The topic for mission study that year was "The Negro." The leaders began to make plans to study the Negro in darkest Africa and the Negro in the deepest South. But one of the ladies had a different idea. "We have forty thousand Negroes right here in our own city," she said. "Why not find out something about them and see what we can do as their Christian fellow citizens?"

As a consequence, a study was undertaken of the local situation, visits were made to some of the Negro churches of the city, and friendships were formed with some of their outstanding women. Finally a project was conceived that involved not only giving money but also rendering personal service to those close at hand who needed friendly advice and moral support. That group of women were getting ahead in their concept of missionary work.

Many of our fellow Americans have been helped to get ahead in a new way of life by means of ventures that even the church is disposed to write down as failures. A little Italian mission was started years ago in a small New Jersey city. After a few years it was abandoned. "It is a waste of money," the executive said. Some years later I encountered a colporteur distributing tracts and Bibles among the Italians in a Colorado mining town. This zealous soul said that he had been converted in that little mission in northern New Jersey. Subsequently, I fell into conversation with one of the officers of an Italian Protestant church in Rochester, New York. He told me that he got his start in the Christian life by reading a tract someone had given him in a mining town in Colorado. Years afterwards I was in Sicily visiting some of the little Protestant congregations there. One of the leaders spoke English, and he told me that during ten years of residence in America he had lived in Rochester, where he had come under the influence of an Italian Protestant church, chiefly through the efforts of one particularly zealous church officer. What a glorious failure that little mission in New Jersey proved to be!

A large church located in a fashionable section of one of our cities for years conducted a "mission" in an unfashionable "foreign" area nearby. A new pastor decided to abandon the mission and have all the people come to the one church. One day an indignant dowager confronted him.

"Do you mean to tell me, Doctor, that I have to sit in the same pew with those dirty foreigners?" she exploded.

"I mean to tell you that this church is open to all who want to come, whoever they may be, and I am sure that our people will give all a Christian welcome," was the pastor's reply.

"I don't like it, and I think I shall go to another church," was the parishioner's ultimatum.

"Well," said the pastor, "we would not like to lose you, but I could give you a letter to any of a number of churches in this city where you would never be troubled by the presence of poor and unfashionable people."

12

The lady thought better of her hasty decision to take her letter, and several months later she was seen at a church social passing ice cream to some of those "foreigners." She was getting ahead—not very far ahead—but still ahead.

But another church in a different city revealed quite another behavior pattern. This wealthy church is located not far from a colony of Mexicans. The furnace in a large Protestant church ministering to the Mexicans broke down one Saturday night in midwinter. A telephone call to the minister of the church on the avenue asking permission for the Mexican congregation to hold their service there that Sunday afternoon brought this response: "Well, I don't know about that. Our people will be afraid that the nice new cushions in our pews will be soiled or even infested." The inquiring pastor slammed down his telephone. His congregation shivered through their service that afternoon in a heatless building. The church on the avenue remained uncontaminated—or did it?

All over the country churches are steering their young people into lives of service, leading them to turn their backs upon the allurements of material success in the city. Furthermore, the churches are inducing those who have attained position and wealth to dedicate themselves and their resources to the service of mankind.

One morning some years ago a young man appeared at the door of L'Institut Français Évangélique in the heart of the French Canadian province of Quebec. The lad had never been to school. He did not know how to read or write. He had no money. He was accepted as a pupil in the primary class at age eighteen. Today that impoverished student has become a leading lawyer in Quebec, is supporting generously the Protestant work in that difficult field, and has a son serving as a minister in the United Church of Canada.

Many of our city churches conduct summer camps for underprivileged children. College men and women are recruited to serve as counselors. Often these young college students derive as much benefit from the summer's experience as do the children. At one such camp a brilliant young student served as counselor for three years. He was working for his Ph.D. and was destined for a position in a private school or college. He was not a church member. But the experience of working with needy boys and discovering how responsive they can be, and the definitely religious atmosphere of the camp, turned this young man's life about radically and completely.

First, he joined the church. A few days before, he wrote to the head counselor: "I want you to be thinking of me next Sunday. For in the cynical atmosphere of this graduate school it takes courage for me to go down to that church and be baptized publicly. I would never have done it had it not been for camp." Later he said: "After my experience at camp I'll never be satisfied unless I am working with underprivileged boys either here or in some foreign field."

Today, equipped with his Ph.D., he is a member of the faculty of a school that takes only needy boys who give promise of Christian leadership. This young man will never make much money, he will never gain rank among the noted scholars, but he is getting ahead.

All too many Protestant churches think they are getting ahead when they run away from difficult situations and

14

strange populations and follow "their own people" to greener pastures. The minister of a church in a definitely slum area of one of our cities found that next door to his church there was a distribution center for narcotic drugs, down the street was a house of prostitution, while across the street the numbers racket was going strong. When he called in the police captain for advice as to how best to clean up the block, the pastor was astonished at the officer's reaction: "Reverend, why don't you get off this block? This is no place for a church." That particular minister was not minded to get off the block, for he had an idea that it was just such places and just such people that Jesus, the friend of the lowly and the outcast, would have us serve. Protestant churches in the city need to get much further ahead in their ministry to the people who need the church and its program most sorely. The parts of our cities where poverty, congestion, delinquency, and crime are flourishing are just the places where the church ought to be, and in strength.

The suburban churches of our nation are apt to be among the strongest, as we shall see. They are also peculiarly subject to the danger of a comfortable, complacent self-sufficiency. Their resources of leadership and money are not always developed to the utmost in the service of the Kingdom. It is encouraging therefore when we hear of a wealthy suburbanite, stimulated by his minister, who organized an information service on the motion pictures scheduled to be shown from week to week in the local theater, so that thoughtful parents may know how to answer when their children clamor: "Let's go to the movies!" It is heart warming to have a report of another layman, supported by his pastor, who helped to organize in his suburb a Community Council wherein all the resources of the community, all the churches, the schools, the Y.M.C.A., the settlement house, and the police force, are pooled in a systematic effort to develop a well rounded program of leisure time activity for their young people. The recent highly publicized stories of juvenile delinquency and crime in some of our privileged suburban communities point up the fact that antisocial behavior is not confined to the city slums. Our well-to-do residential churches need to be getting ahead in their program for their own young people.

How surely the patient and sympathetic guidance of a true Christian can help young people to get ahead on the right path! A young Negro girl from a broken home was a problem child both in school and in church. But the church leader was very patient. No matter how the girl misbehaved, the leader never gave up. The average teacher would have thrown out the youngster in exasperation, but not this one. She asked the girl to her home. She invited her for lunch. She gave her responsibility. Realizing that the girl had real musical ability (she wanted to be a "blues singer"), the leader gave her a lead in the choir. She took her to camp and gave her responsibility, first as junior counselor and then as counselor. As she grew older, she was given charge of a girls' club. The young and ambitious girl thrived under confidence given and responsibility bestowed.

Today that girl, having finished her college training in religious education, is the director of a program that enlists 6,000 youngsters monthly, the program director of a summer camp of 270 boys and girls, and the leader of a chorus of 200 voices. She might have had her name blazoned in neon lights as a singer in a night club. Instead her name and her personality light up the faces and warm the hearts of thousands of Negro boys and girls. She is getting ahead.

This business of getting ahead in the Christian way is not always easy. There are so many forces in our city life at work to push people down and to pervert their ideas of the meaning of life. Here is the testimony of a thoughtful student who is at work in one of the nation's worst slums:

I have a youngster six years old in my group. He is one of the most sensitive, intelligent boys I have ever known. But, at the same time, he is a child of fears and twisted emotions. In a group he can be a terror; when we walk off our block he grips my hand and sticks close to my side. One day he confided in me. His father lives away; his mother is "on welfare." Three tiny rooms house four children and their mother. In the hallway outside sleep three bums—"drunk mans," he calls them. The boy finds it hard to get to Sunday school at 10:30 because his mother plays cards all Saturday night and won't wake him. Across the rubbish filled vacant lot from his building is a hole of a candy store which, according to Frank, "pushes dope." Sex? This six year old boy has told me stories that would burn your faces. Where does he get his ideas of right and wrong? Well, right to him is anything that pays off for him. Wrong is anything that hurts. His code is the survival of the fittest. To such an environment, to such a code this six-year-old is already a slave.

To get ahead in such a neighborhood is to be a member of the strongest gang, then its leader, then a gangster or dope peddler. And the end of that is prison, and at the end of that, too often, is more crime.

To get ahead in such city areas the church must do more

17

than preach—much more. It has to understand the problems of these slum-perverted youngsters and their parents, learn to get on with them, win their confidence and respect, and, with them, do battle against those social conditions that drag young and old down to the depths and keep them there.

. . . *The City's Missionary Task*

This, then, is one of the fundamental missionary tasks in the city—setting people on the Christian path and giving them the drive to push ahead on it and proving to the often heartless city that it has a soul and that it had better see to it that it is saved. Local churches of all kinds are at work at this task as well as the specifically city missionary agencies. Our large city churches, our strong suburban churches, our average medium sized churches, our foreign language churches, our mission churches—all have a part to play. Much of the constructive work in our American cities is done by little known churches and by unpublicized ministers. We need a re-evaluation of what constitutes a great city church.

The situation in our cities calls for a much greater amount of teamwork between churches, within denominations, and across denominational lines, as we shall see. Much energy and devoted consecration is being given to this task, but no one would say that our city churches are addressing themselves to the task at hand with such vigor and imaginative foresight as the situation demands.

The American city throbs with dynamic energy, much of

18

it directed to materialistic ends by secular minded people. It is high time that the spiritual forces of the city exhibit an equally dynamic drive devoted to spiritual ends. America cannot afford to have the churches of its cities dwarfed and overshadowed by the skyscraping symbols of purely materialistic achievement, for America and the world need a dynamic and vital religious faith and we have a right to look to our cities for an expression of it.

two | THE LONELINESS OF
CITY PEOPLE

"I was a stranger . . ."

IT IS a little town, a mere hamlet of less than five hundred inhabitants. It might be in Vermont or Pennsylvania or Kansas or Texas or Colorado. John and Mary are sitting on the front porch, if it is summer, or in the front room in cold weather (one at each window). The day's work is done, the meager supper consumed. So they sit down to rest. There is little conversation, but there is usually a comment on each passer-by, for they know them all and can identify them even when they speed by at fifty miles an hour.

"That's Elmer—he's late today."

"There goes Aunt Emmy on the way to Violet's house." A stranger comes along. "Who's that man?"

"He must be the one who's bought the Thomas place."

Their eyes follow the stranger until he is out of sight. Then Mary gets up and goes to the party line telephone. Before she rings off, she knows all that anyone in the village knows about the newcomer. Be his reputation good, bad, or indifferent, the coming of the stranger to their town is an event, and he and his family and his affairs will provide conversation for weeks to come.

A stranger comes to the city—any large city. He steps out of the railway terminal onto the busy street. He stands there bewildered for a moment. Then he stops one of the hurrying passers-by.

"Can you tell me how to get to Union Avenue?"

"I'm sorry, Mister, I'm a stranger here myself," is the reply he most often receives.

. . .   *Alone in the Big City*

There you have in a nutshell one difference between rural and urban communities. In the one a stranger is an exception; in the other most of the people are strangers to one another. They may be newcomers, visitors, commuters, or people acquainted with but one section of the city or one segment of the population. In the country everyone knows everyone else; in the city if you meet a friend on the street it is an event.

In the smaller cities, of course, the rural pattern obtains, for they are but overgrown small towns, and on Main Street you are liable to meet many people you know. But let the city grow, as most do, and you find people saying to one another, "I used to know almost everyone in this town (or in this church), but now I hardly ever see a familiar face."

In the town and in the smaller city, a large proportion of the people are relatively permanent residents. Life-long friendships have a chance to develop. Marriages take place between young people who have grown up together in the same community as playmates and schoolmates. Even when they move away to larger cities, this town is still the old home, and on their visits they are welcomed back by old friends and neighbors.

This security that comes from old associations is lacking in the city, and the larger the city the more glaring is that lack. The city is full of friendless folk. The city dweller may be rich in acquaintances, but he is poor in the tested and tried friendships that act as a stabilizing influence in times of crisis. People are surrounded by crowds, but their social contacts with one another are very limited. In the city an individual has to make an effort to find acquaintances and make friends by joining groups centering about his work or engaging in extracurricular activities in clubs, lodges, community organizations, educational and social groups, or churches. Casual acquaintances are rare. Neighborliness is almost nonexistent. One can live ten years in a city apartment and have but a bowing acquaintance with the folks above or across the hall.

The old neighborhoods that used to bind people together with a sense of community tend to disappear as cities grow larger and life in them becomes more complex. It is true that even in the largest of cities there are still neighborhoods based on the stores that minister to the essential needs of the residents: the grocery store, the drugstore, the laundry, the dry cleaning establishment, etc. When a city dweller leaves for an extended stay, the proprietors of these stores are the only ones who miss him and the only ones to welcome him on his return. His associations are not made on the basis of location but on the basis of community interests. Thus the real community of the city dweller may be scattered all over the city and even out into the suburbs.

If this situation makes the normal city dweller an anonymous individual, freed from the stabilization of friendships and the restraints of the opinion of neighbors, it wreaks havoc with the lives of those less favored by circumstances. The aged, the failures, the slipping, and the unadjustable people of our cities are all too apt to be unutterably lonely and lost in the midst of the unheeding multitudes.

Recently whole new cities have sprung up in housing projects or about defense projects. To a consideration of their problems we shall turn in a later chapter. In these instances, at least, everyone is on the same footing. They are all strangers. All can make their adjustments together.

. . .   *Strangers and Foreigners*

In most American cities there are groups that are strangers by virtue of a national, racial, or cultural background differing from that of the dominant Anglo-Saxon group of old line Americans. In Burlington, Vermont, or Lewiston, Maine, it is the French Canadians; in New Bedford, the Portuguese; in New York, the Italians, the Jews, the Puerto Ricans, the Negroes (and any other group you care to name); in Chicago, the Czechs, Poles, Mexicans, and Negroes; in San Antonio and Los Angeles, the Mexicans; in Albuquerque, New Mexico, the Indians; in San Francisco, the Chinese; in Seattle, the Japanese. These groups include many who are real strangers to American life, as were the Germans, the Scandinavians, the Irish, and the Italians a generation or two ago.

All such groups upon their arrival are prone to colonize in a given section of the city. Thus we have had our German, Irish, Swedish, and Norwegian colonies, our little Italys, our Jewish ghettoes, as we have today our San Juan in the Subway, our Harlem and its equivalent, our Mexican town, our Chinatown. These groups are accused of clannishness. But this flocking together is natural and inevitable at the outset of their life in our cities. Strangers to American life and to the English language, they inevitably congregate where they can associate freely with people whose customs and language they understand and among whom they feel at home.

These colonies often resemble real communities. In no part of our city life is neighborliness and mutual helpfulness more evident. But they are shut out from the main stream of American life, partly because of barriers of language and custom, partly because of the bars put up by prejudice and discriminating practices.

The great epic of American life has been the integration into our common life of people who came to us as Germans, as Irish, as Swedes, as Czechs, as Italians, or as Jews and who are now Americans in every sense. Who ever thinks of a Willkie or an Eisenhower as a German? But the task that we have performed so magnificently with the early immigrant groups now has to be completed with other groups— Orientals, Spanish-speaking people, Negroes, and in a more limited degree with displaced persons and foreign students.

The displaced persons who have been brought here since the close of World War II are relatively small in number, but they have been cast into the seething maelstrom of the life of many of our great cities. Victims of the war, bombed out, incarcerated for months in concentration camps, many of them well along in years, is it any wonder that they of all our new arrivals find themselves bewildered, confused, and frustrated by the hurry and bustle and apparent heartlessness of city people? Nor are our natives universally appreciative of having these displaced persons placed in their communities. I heard one lady who prides herself upon her membership in the Mayflower Society complaining bitterly about the inundation of her neighborhood with displaced persons. She was quite unconscious of the fact that those who came to these shores on the Mayflower were the original displaced persons. And what a precious cargo they brought with them!

> Laws, freedom, truth, and faith in God
> Came with those exiles o'er the waves.

Who knows what enrichment of American life may result from the contribution of these latest arrivals, battered though they have been by some of the most cruel experiences mankind has ever had to endure?

Another small but very important group is composed of foreign students. These young potential leaders of the countries of Europe, Asia, and Africa, brought here under governmental, private, and even church auspices, are scattered throughout our university campuses. Too many are left to shift for themselves and to find out for themselves what America is like. The impressions thus gathered and the interpretations consequently made by these students in their homelands are often unfortunate and have been at times disastrous to the cause of international good will. We need to show a little simple friendliness, opening American homes to such students. Their exposure to the finest and best that this country has to offer in our homes, in our churches, and in our cultural institutions, and above all, the building of real friendship, will mean much to the cause of international good will.

When a young German leader has in this country those whom he calls "my American parents," he is bound to approach the whole question of Germany's place in the world and her attitude toward the West in a different spirit than if he had had no such warm personal relationships.

A Negro student from Sierra Leone had his whole impression of America transformed by a friendly experience in a suburban home near his university. He afterwards stated: "When Americans tell our people that they are really working at a solution of the race problem, they will think it is propaganda. But when I go back and tell them of my experience they will believe me."

. . .   *Who Are "Our Kind of People"?*

The factor of prejudice raises its ugly head in our relationships with the Orientals, the Spanish-speaking group, and the Negroes. We act as if we want to keep these groups separate, segregated, and "in their place" at the bottom of the social and economic ladder.

An Italian immigrant, who is now a Ph.D. and a college

professor, has written a penetrating analysis of the difference between America and his native Italy.

The Italian principle . . . was predicated upon the view . . . that privilege is hereditary and the exclusive possession of the few. It excluded the bulk of men from all but the barest material necessities, but also from the possibility of achievement and enjoyment in the realm of the mind. The American principle, on the other hand . . . encouraged all men to the adventure of achievement and enjoyment in all realms, each according to his own capacity. . . . For in America it is believed that man is worth perfecting, that human life is sacred . . . and that man therefore . . . has the right to grow, to mature, and to die in dignity rather than disgrace.[1]

We can rejoice that so many who have come lately to our shores and dwelt in our cities have come to share Pellegrini's appreciation of the true American way of life. But do we really recognize the right of *all* men to self-realization? Do we recognize that right for the Oriental, the Mexican, the Negro? We are making a beginning, but it is as yet a small beginning, and in this movement the churches of America, and more especially the city churches, lag far behind. Eleven o'clock on Sunday morning is the most segregated hour in America. For the most part, Orientals, Mexicans, Puerto Ricans, Indians, and Negroes gather to worship by themselves. We are far from practicing in our churches the brotherhood we preach. In fact, we are far from practicing the friendliness and neighborliness we espouse.

For many city churches give the appearance of being exclusive spiritual clubs for "our kind of people." Some are

[1] *The Immigrant's Return*, by Angelo M. Pellegrini, pp. 260 ff. New York, The Macmillan Co., 1951. Used by permission.

not even friendly to strangers of "their own kind." A friend of mine, a good churchman, moved to a new suburban community. He and his wife shopped around for a new church home. He reports that in instance after instance the members of the congregation were too busy greeting one another to pay any attention to strangers, and the couple left with never a welcoming word from anyone. They persevered and finally made a church home for themselves, but less devoted Christians would have been frozen out after a few attempts.

. . .   *Churches That Make Friends*

On the other hand, a church in a suburb of Detroit has grown by leaps and bounds by the simple expedient of seeing to it that strangers are welcomed, their names and addresses taken, and the family called upon by the pastor that very afternoon.

A newcomer to a Chicago suburb established a casual contact with a young married couples' group that met every two weeks in one another's homes. Within the next two weeks three or four members of the group telephoned his home with pressing invitations for him and his wife to attend the next gathering. As a result, the couple made so many friends that they were brokenhearted when they had to return to their own home city six months later.

City church parishes are full of lonely people and many a pastor is so immersed in administrative work and in preaching around the country that he has little time or inclination for "bell-ringing." And yet one pastor stumbled on a case like this: A florist in his congregation had been specializing

28

for years on pansies and had developed an extraordinarily large and beautiful flower. Then came disaster—an unsuccessful operation for cataracts and total blindness. The pastor found him sitting alone in the middle of his empty greenhouse, worrying about how to realize on his property. That one visit alone, and its follow-up, were worth a dozen committee meetings.

Our city churches have paid all too little attention to the problem of the aged, now such a rapidly increasing element in our population. So many are lonely and frustrated or victims of various kinds of "senile delinquency." Pastoral visitation of the elderly means more than most ministers will ever realize. But why could not more churches organize recreational and craft programs for the oldsters? They have the space; leadership can be found among the old people themselves; all that is needed is a little initiative and guidance on the part of the church. The church was instrumental in starting the Y.M.C.A., the Y.W.C.A., and young people's conferences. Why not an old men's Christian association and old people's conferences or their equivalent? Public and private welfare agencies are pioneering in this service. The church should not be left behind. As a matter of fact, some very significant enterprises have recently been inaugurated by local city churches, known variously as The Golden Age Club, The Three Score and Ten Club, Friendly Folks, The Oldsters. Denominational boards on both the national and the local level, notably the Methodist and the Episcopal, are beginning actively to promote programs aimed at this age group.

In 1953 a most significant interdenominational Confer-

29

ence on the Church and Older Persons was held under the auspices of the Division of Christian Education of the National Council of the Churches of Christ in the U. S. A. The findings of this conference have just been published in a pamphlet entitled, "The Fulfillment Years in Christian Education—A Program for Older Persons." [1] In it there are definite and concrete suggestions for a program in a local church designed to meet the spiritual, social, and psychological needs of older people. One would expect that this will be one of the great forward steps in programizing in local city churches in the years immediately ahead.

There was a time in our cities when our churches could carry on "missions" for the poor and "foreign" elements at a safe distance from the church. Now many of the colonies are breaking up and the second and third generations of immigrants are scattered over the city so that many a city church finds them right under the eaves of their own building. The home church must become a missionary society, dedicated to reaching all in its immediate community who are not in vital contact with organized religion. But no! They are not "our kind of people." So young Italians justify the continuance of so-called "Italian churches" because "we are not made welcome in the American churches." So Mexicans and Japanese who have prospered and moved out to the suburbs hesitate to join a nearby church lest they be rebuffed because of their color. So Negroes stick to Negro churches partly because they are nearby and familiar, but partly because they know how they will be received in white churches.

[1] Published by the Division of Christian Education, National Council of Churches, 79 E. Adams St., Chicago, Ill. 50 cents.

A band of Iroquois Indians who winter in one of our Eastern cities found a welcome in a small city church. They now call it The-Church-That-Makes-Friends. No wonder!—for besides the Indians, you will find at a Sunday morning service Puerto Ricans, Italians, Syrians, and Negroes, all worshiping and working together.

A church located near a public housing project found that Negroes were moving in. The church had successively ministered to Germans, Italians, Chinese, Russians, and Puerto Ricans—but this was something new. "What shall I do?" the pastor queried. His officers were quick in their reply. "We have always ministered to the people in this community no matter who they were. That is still our policy." Today in that church and in its Sunday school are to be found all the national and racial groups in the neighborhood, including of course a goodly proportion of Negroes. No wonder the Jews of the neighborhood say of this pastor, "He not only preaches brotherhood; he makes brotherhood walk in our streets and climb our tenement house stairs."

On the West Coast a church building left vacant by the tragic evacuation of the Japanese during the war has now become the scene of a splendid demonstration of an inclusive ministry. Among the 100 members of the church, there are 32 Negroes, 32 Japanese, 30 Caucasians, 2 Chinese, 2 Koreans, and 2 Filipinos. The pastor shows the spirit that animates this enterprise in this declaration: "I want it clearly understood that this is not an 'interracial' church. We are just a church. A church that is Christian must have its doors open to all. We have not organized this church because we are fed up with segregation. We have organized it because

31

we all believe in Christ and have grown up to the point where we feel at ease with Christians of other ethnic and racial stock."

It is in our cities that Christians have the greatest opportunity for firsthand contact with Christians of other ethnic and racial stock. Where but in the churches would we expect people to grow up to the point where they will feel at ease with Christians of other backgrounds?

We have much to learn from the sects and their store front churches at this point. Here is an informal atmosphere, a meeting room easily accessible, no iron gates nor oaken doors to crash, no frock coated ushers to impress and overawe, just a simple, warm friendliness and welcoming place for the humblest, no matter what his color or what his dress.

Must we continue always having segregated Japanese and Chinese churches when our Orientals are gradually being dispersed throughout the country and are ready in language, education, and economic status to take their place beside other Americans on a parity?

Must the churches conform to the pattern of segregation and discrimination prevailing wherever Mexicans and Puerto Ricans congregate? True, there is a language barrier here that necessitates separate services for the adults. But the children and young people soon learn English. Why cannot they be absorbed in nearby American churches? Are Mexicans always to be the hewers of wood and drawers of water —despised, menial laborers for whom a "mission" is good enough?

And what of our Negro churches? In many a northern city they are among our strongest churches numerically. But

Protestants are still far from an aggressive and statesmanlike ministry to the Negroes of our cities. The white Protestants either leave the Negro churches alone on the theory that they know best how to organize and run their churches, or we condescendingly tender a little aid here and there to help Negro churches over a tough spot. It is high time that white and Negro churches learned how to work together in a statesmanlike ministry to this important group so strongly Protestant in their heritage and inclination. In survey after survey of city church situations it is brought out that the Negro churches are isolated geographically and organizationally from the main currents of Protestant life.

The solution does not lie entirely in interracial churches, though clearly there is room for more such inclusive churches ministering to the people of the community whoever they are. But the solution does lie in the recognition of the fact that here is one of the neediest groups in our cities, one with high potentialities and one with much to contribute to the Protestant forces of our cities. It is high time that they are brought into the church family as fullfledged members and not left standing outside the door, strangers to the best that America has to offer.

If we reach out in sincere friendship for all those within reach, whoever they may be, and extend a warm welcome within the church, there will be fewer strangers in our cities, fewer lonely souls, and more churches filled with people whose hearts have been warmed and whose souls have been enlarged by the ministry of the church.

three | THE CITIES AND PEOPLE

ON THE MOVE

*"He went out, not knowing
where he was to go"*

THE history of civilization and the role of religion therein, and, more especially, the history of America and the role of religion in American life, can be told in terms of the migrations of people, as individuals and in the mass.

That part of human history which is recorded in the Bible is illustrative of this fact. We see Abraham going out, not knowing whither he went, but becoming under God the father of Israel; Moses leading the children of Israel out of Egypt into the promised land; Ruth expressing her loyalty to Naomi in the immortal words, "Where you go I will go . . . your people shall be my people and your God my God"; the exile of the Jews, their return and subsequent dispersion.

The story of religion can be told in terms of people moving, motivated by faith or carrying their faith or lack of it with them as a part of their baggage, and accommodating that faith to the conditions prevailing in the new homeland.

34

The history of America is based on migrations and may be told in terms of the explorers, hunters, trappers, frontiersmen, backwoodsmen, traders, and homesteaders, the covered wagons, the slave ships, and immigrants, the displaced persons of all lands and all generations. This is the saga of America—people on the move, pushing out our frontiers, settling over vast expanses of land, making use of the unparalleled natural resources of this great continent. The history of religion in America may be told in terms of pioneer missionaries, circuit riders, camp meetings, developing churches, and church inspired "log colleges" that developed into great universities.

This movement of the American people has been tremendously accelerated throughout the past century with the sensational development of the means of public communication. The steamboats, the railroads, the improved mail service, the telegraph, the telephone, the automobile, the airplane, motion pictures, radio, and television have all had an enormous contributing influence in the growth of cities and in the extent of their influence upon the life of the country. For as a result of these facilities, it is now an easy and simple matter for people to flock to our cities in response to the American drive to get ahead. Moreover, ideas, too, have become more mobile, so that the type of life, the standards and ideas generated in the city can be easily and quickly communicated to the rest of the country and become formative in our entire national life.

But within the past ten years, accelerated by the demands

of the industrial effort during World War II and by the present prodigious defense program, the American people are on the move to an extent and in a manner unprecedented in our history.

People are moving from the country to the city, from the city to the suburbs, from one part of the country to another to an unprecedented degree. No less than 13,000,000 people changed their state of residence between 1940 and 1950, and 70,000,000 moved at least once during this period. Twenty per cent of the people in the United States changed their addresses during the past year and in parts of our cities the percentage has been much higher as new housing developments have gone up, slum areas have been cleared of their ancient buildings, and new transportation facilities have opened up outlying areas for residential purposes and made others more accessible.

This moving about only accentuates the fluidity of city life as the tide of urban population throughout the city flows east and west, north and south, in and out, up and down. Into the offices and factories in the morning, out on the streets at noon, crowding into buses, trolleys, automobiles, and subways at the end of the workday, and back to the theater district in the evening move the city crowds, always in a hurry, always trying to keep up with the inexorable time schedule that dominates life in the city.

This normal hypermobility of the city's population has been accentuated by the mobilization of the defense effort of the nation in recent years. In general, the population trend has been westward to the West Coast and the Southwest, where many of the great defense plants have been located and where the cities have recorded the most phenomenal growth.

In Texas, Arizona, New Mexico, Colorado, and especially in California the growth of old cities and the mushroom growth of new urban communities has been astounding. While the population of the country as a whole was doubled between 1900 and 1950, that of the Pacific Coast region has increased 500 per cent.

The population growth in California and in particular Southern California has been phenomenal. The building permits issued in the first five months of 1953 tell the story. The staggering totals are:

The West Coast (outside of California)	$160,268,314
Northern California	158,606,189
Southern California (outside of Los Angeles County)	277,176,763
Los Angeles County	483,707,499

The population in Los Angeles County has increased from 2,785,623 in 1940 to 4,151,687 in 1950 and an estimated 4,600,000 in 1953. This may be concreted in terms of the increase between 1940 and 1950 in a few communities in Los Angeles County selected at random: Van Nuys 20,298 to 57,053; Pacoima 7,248 to 24,301; Duarte 2,198 to 13,267; Encino 1,548 to 10,832; Sepulveda 2,502 to 11,598. Vacant lots and truck gardens are covered with acres of new houses. Tiny communities have mushroomed into fullfledged cities. These new developments, new houses, and new families all call for new churches. No wonder denominational officials are clamoring for funds to take advantage of this opportunity for an extended ministry to these new communities. Assign-

37

ments of responsibility are made by the Council of Churches and are taken up as fast as financial resources permit.

. . .　　　　　　　　*Our New Defense Communities*

Quite sensational in size and scope and its social and religious implications have been the development of new defense plants and new residential communities for the workers.

The Atomic Energy Commission decided to locate a large plant for the manufacture of hydrogen bombs in the Savannah River Valley. An area covering 315 square miles was selected for that purpose, not far from Augusta, Georgia.

This had been a quiet, serene Southern countryside dotted with tiny villages and given over to the growing of cotton and peanuts. But now all of a sudden some 40,000 workers were brought in to build the plant. These construction workers and their families crowded into Augusta, doubling its population almost overnight, and took up their abode in huge trailer camps. The once peaceful Carolina roads were jammed with cars rushing to and from the enormous atomic installation. At the same time eleven mammoth power dams were being built on the Savannah River; an old army camp nearby was reactivated and the personnel at Augusta Arsenal greatly increased.

These workers came from all over the country and most of them brought their families with them. A large number will be there only temporarily during the construction of the plant, but many will remain in the area as workmen, supervisors, and executives in the plant.

38

One can scarcely imagine how utterly swamped the social resources of that countryside have been. How to house these thousands of newcomers, how to provide schooling for the children, adequate roads for the cars, and hospital care for the sick was a problem of the first magnitude. Outside Augusta, the only churches available were little rural churches. The problem of arranging for worship services and pastoral care was immediate and pressing. Newcomers needed help and advice in getting established. Recreational and fellowship activities for young and old, family counseling, and even financial aid for disappointed job seekers were crying needs.

To meet these emergent needs the Division of Home Missions of the National Council of Churches was able to mobilize the resources of the denominations through its Committee on Ministry to Defense Communities. Personnel has been thrown into the area, temporary churches established in halls, mortuaries, tents, and trailers, and plans devised for permanent and adequate church buildings.

Scarcely less dramatic and urgent was the situation that developed at another atomic energy development sixteen miles west of Paducah, Kentucky. The population of that city is expected to become stabilized at 100,000, as compared with its 1950 population of 32,430. All of the surrounding villages have been similarly bloated. All normal facilities are lacking. There were neither schools, churches, clubs, health, nor recreational facilities. The newly arrived families were overwhelmed by a complex of personal and social problems.

Here the local churches of Paducah have mobilized for

action with a fine demonstration of unity in the face of an emergency. Again the Committee on Defense Communities has been able to call upon the denominational boards for help, which has been promptly and generously given. An equally challenging situation is developing in the Scioto Valley in Ohio.

The experience in these and earlier defense communities, such as Oak Ridge, Tennessee, and Los Alamos, New Mexico, has demonstrated that the Protestant churches can rise to an emergency and that they can join forces to meet a crisis.

Fast Action Called For

These exceptional emergent situations have galvanized the churches into action by their dramatic giantism and the very evident need for speedy and united action. The churches have had to move immediately and establish their contacts with these workers speedily, for many of them would be gone before the slow processes of ecclesiastical deliberation came to fruition.

A minister once established in a situation like this has to move quickly. One who has led a congregation at Oak Ridge, Tennessee, through the hectic years of the development of that community reports that in six years he has received 1,000 members, many of whom have since been transferred to churches elsewhere. He underlines the absolute necessity of visiting newcomers constantly, impressing on them the value of uniting with the local church even if they are only to be in the community temporarily. He aims to give them something to do in and for the church immediately and plans regular fellowship gatherings so that new families may become acquainted with one another. If these families then leave, they are apt to carry with them to their new home the idea that the church can and should occupy a large place in their lives.

. . .   *Other New Communities*

Other new cities are arising that are apt to be of a more permanent nature but that constitute the same sort of a challenge to the churches. The erection of the new Fairless plant of the United States Steel Company at Morrisville, Pennsylvania, has necessitated the creation in that rural area of a new city with a population of 75,000. A large part of this is being built and managed by Levitt and Sons and will be known as Levittown. This community is planned by that company down to the last shrub and will include facilities for educational, health, and recreational needs. Lots have been set aside for churches and the assignment of responsibility has been made interdenominationally through the Philadelphia Council of Churches. Here again the denominations must act quickly to get their churches built and to establish contacts with the residents as soon as possible after they move in.

All of these instances are dramatic, and they command action by their very size and evident emergency. But the mobility of the population in the ordinary city calls for the same sort of speed on the part of the churches.

Let a new housing project—public or private—go up in

41

one of our cities and the Roman Catholic Church springs into action immediately. If there is not a Roman Catholic Church nearby, one is built, and perhaps a parish house and parochial school besides. Meantime, the nearby Protestant churches go into endless committee meetings trying to decide what to do and how to do it, and several years elapse before any of them have either plant or staff or program equal to the new situation. If a minister should follow the moving van into these new apartments and take his place along with the salesmen of household appliances, he would be likely to gain the attention and interest of the newcomers in the program of his church. But if months and years go by without any Protestant minister or church member showing any interest in the new resident and his spiritual welfare, he wi'l find it very easy to establish a pattern of life with religion occupying a very insignificant place.

. . .   *What Moving Does to People*

Each time a family moves, a new pattern of life is formed. New friends are made, new associations formed, new daily and weekly schedules made out. Even those who were church people in their former home will find it very easy to fall into a Sunday schedule of a lazy morning with the newspaper, an afternoon with friends, and an evening at the movies, and a week day schedule that is entirely devoid of religious references.

We must remember that millions of our fellow citizens have had their social roots torn up. They cannot carry their roots with them. New roots have to be put down with each move in new soil. When you plant radishes or carrots you cannot pull them up every day or so, plant them in another place, and expect them to grow. Yet we expect America's moving millions to flourish after their transplantation, and to a surprising degree they are doing so.

People who move as often as our city folk develop the psychology of transiency. They are here today and gone tomorrow. So why try to put down roots in their present place of residence? They will only have to repeat the painful process of uprooting themselves again. Accordingly, let life be made up of one's work, one's amusement, and such friendships as may be quickly cultivated and easily broken off.

. . . *What Moving Does to Churches*

In the midst of this moving procession stand the churches. By nature and by tradition they are stable institutions with a program designed for a stable population. Such a program is adequate for churches made up largely of settled parishioners, who own their own homes and expect to bring up their children in the community. But in apartment house areas and in the tenement houses of the slums "the gospel army must be trained to shoot on the wing," as one home mission report puts it.

We have not adjusted either our program or our psychology to that situation. We do not move fast enough to reach people when they move in, nor do we make sufficient effort to see to it that the ministry of the church follows people when they move out. One denomination reports that 30 per cent of its membership is absentee. If those out of town members are just carried on the rolls and no effort is made to locate them in churches in their new communities within *the first year*, the probability is that they will be lost to the church. By the same token, as departed members are relocated in church homes, newcomers must be won to an active interest in the church in the first year of their residence, or they probably will never be won.

One city pastor states that when he came to his parish he could find only one third of those whose names were on the roll. The rest had moved away, were not followed up promptly, and had disappeared into the limbo of those whom the post office classifies as "moved—address unknown." In the poorer sections of the cities the losses are even greater. If people are relocated by a housing authority, for example, they may be given twenty-four hours' notice to pack up and move; they have no time to notify friends of the church as to where they are going, and they are not letter writers.

. . . . *Negro and Spanish-speaking Migrants*

This psychology of transiency is the more marked where a radical change of environment is involved in the people's moves. When Negroes move from the South to our Northern cities and industrial centers as they have been doing by the hundreds of thousands, the following adjustments have to be made: (1) from a predominantly rural or small town culture and an agricultural economy to an urban metropolitan culture and an industrial-commercial economy; (2) from rural and small town slums to urban slums; (3) from

44

a rigid caste system of racial relationships to a less well defined, more impersonal, but about equally burdensome system of discrimination against the Negro; (4) from a personal social restriction to an impersonal system of residential isolation and vocational and social discrimination.

The urban Negro finds himself a victim of the mass resentment engendered by his ghetto living. He is subjected to the pressure of a complex mechanistic society on an already suppressed sense of individuality. He is made more acutely conscious of the race problem as it presses upon him. He is subject to the efforts of many pressure groups to capitalize on his race feeling to wean him away from traditional loyalties. The forces of secularism, radical political movements both of the right and the left, the aggressive missionary program of the Roman Catholic Church, the lure of the cults, all set to work on the transplanted Negro. The stabilizing influence of community life is weakened as he finds himself one of a great mass of individuals driven this way and that by the winds of strange influences and doctrines.

The Puerto Ricans in New York and the Mexicans in the Southwest and California face all the familiar problems of immigrants: crowded slum housing, low paid jobs, language difficulties, prejudices and ghetto-living, health hazards, the alienation of the second generation, schools and social agencies not adapted to their needs.

The progress made by the Spanish-speaking groups in the face of these problems has been remarkable. They have proved themselves to be a highly adaptable people, quick to learn and to adjust. But again the churches and social agencies are offering a program that is too little and too late.

45

Such Protestant work as has been initiated among the Negroes and the Spanish-speaking people has been too largely confined to evangelism and worship. In all too few instances is this program supplemented by educational, welfare, and recreational activities and services. The moral and spiritual welfare of children and young people is neglected even in some of the strongest of the churches ministering to these groups. Again, the churches must act quickly, before the children from such homes come under antisocial influences and form habit patterns that make them a social menace instead of the constructive element they are capable of being.

. . . *"Shooting on the Wing"*

The effect of the intensified mobility of the people of our American cities upon our churches and their program is far reaching. A Scottish Presbyterian church finds itself surrounded by Jews. An Italian church finds that Negroes are filling its neighborhood. A "mission church" geared to the needs of the poor suddenly finds itself in the midst of the lofty apartments of the rich. A suburban church finds itself inundated by thousands of new people. New suburbs and new cities develop overnight and churches have to be organized and buildings provided. New housing projects, public and private, bring tens of thousands of people within reach of little churches with a membership of two hundred and a budget of $7,500. All these rapidly changing situations call for speedy and radical readjustments and wise planning.

But more important is the need of a spirit of inclusive

46

friendliness that can be put into action speedily. Churches cannot wait for new people to come to them; they must move out after them and without delay. The speedy and effective swinging into action of the churches in the defense communities can and should be emulated in all cities of rapid change. For every ten thousand people who have moved into new homes in these new defense communities, hundreds of thousands are moving into new homes in our older cities and their suburbs. Only by alert and quick adaptation of program can we lead these moving millions to put down roots in their new communities and in the churches of these communities.

THE CITIES AND PEOPLE ON THE MOVE

*"You cleanse the outside
of the cup . . ."*

WHETHER it be in New York or Atlanta, Boston, Seattle, Chicago, Houston, or Los Angeles, the buses that transport us up and down the streets are strategic listening posts from which to hear the voices of city people. Since city voices are apt to be shrill and strident, willy-nilly one overhears conversations.

Two middle-aged ladies of suburban mien were exchanging their views on life in the seat behind me, and this is what one of them had to offer. "When I was a young girl I had dreams of what I hoped life might hold for me: to marry a good man, to have two children, a house of our own in the country, an automobile, a fur coat, and a trip to Europe. Now all these dreams have come true, and I suppose I will have to start looking around to find something else to live for."

Some years ago a popular magazine ran a feature article

that endeavored to pictorialize "The American Dream." In it were portrayed a married couple (Junior executives, probably) standing in front of a $20,000 suburban home, with their two children and their poodle. Out on the front lawn was their late model car, their electric washing machine, dishwasher, vacuum cleaner, refrigerator, television set, and an assorted grouping of other household gadgets. The American dream had come true in the accepted terms of material possessions.

The mail order catalogue is more apt to have the place of honor on the living room table than the Bible. Indeed, more than once it has been seriously proposed that the most effective anti-Communist propaganda would be the dropping of thousands of mail order catalogues upon Communist territory from the air. "See what our free democracy has produced and placed within reach of the common man. Can your regime match that?" So runs the argument to prove our superiority in production.

This emphasis upon the American standard of living expressed in terms of material possession instead of upon an American standard of life expressed in terms of character, ideals, and purposes is characteristic of our culture. But it is in the life of our cities that this externalism is most vividly seen. The very word "urbanity" implies sophistication, worldly wisdom, knowing one's way about in a world of things. A civilized man is by derivation of the word one who lives and thinks in a city. As Canon Bernard Iddings Bell points out in his *Crowd Culture*,[1] such a civilized man could

[1] Pp. 37-38. New York, Harper and Brothers, 1952. Used by permission.

49

be produced only in a city of an earlier age that was "a community, a constant group of families, each of which, and each of whose members, had a stake in the common welfare and was not permitted to forget it." Now, in our larger cities (and only to a lesser extent in our smaller ones) "while there is opportunity to express oneself all over the map, there is next to no neighborhood opinion to exercise correction. Because our mores are no longer determined by mutual consent among friends they are built up mechanically and anonymously . . . our cities have ceased to civilize, have ceased to become communities."

The same exclusive emphasis upon external matters is revealed in some of our highest social aims. We want all of our people to be "well housed, well fed, and well employed," and we announce this aim with such messianic fervor that one is led to believe that all of our problems would be solved if those aims were accomplished. If such were the case, then we might suppose that life on Park Avenue, in Grosse Pointe, on Peachtree Avenue, Sunset Boulevard, or Lake Shore Drive, would resemble that of the heavenly Jerusalem. But moral decadence, superficial living, and unhappy homes are distressingly frequent among the well housed, well fed, and well employed residents of the fashionable sections of our cities. We mistake the physical base of the good life for the good life itself. We confuse the material instrumentalities for living with the ends of life. We know how to conjugate the verb "to have" but not the verb "to be."

Our city dwellers are obsessed with the worship of bigness. "Watch Smithtown Grow" is the slogan of the small city's Chamber of Commerce. "See how tall our buildings are, how capacious our apartment houses, how extensive our public and private housing projects, how gigantic our industrial plants, how enormous our profits, how large our universities, how big our football stadium, and how large and imposing our churches," says the proud city dweller.

. . .   *Externalism*

Halford Luccock in *Jesus and the American Mind* has a whole chapter on "Externalism." [1] In it, he stresses the American tendency to confuse bigness with greatness, to believe that "a thing becomes a hundred times as important if it is a hundred times as big. . . . The city with the greatest population, the store with the greatest sales, the motion picture actor with the largest salary—to us these are objects of awe." Luccock goes on to point out that the significance of life is always to be measured by quality, not by quantity. "Not the size of cities, but the kind of life lived in them; not the mountains of manufactured goods, but the kind of men created in the process; not bank clearings, but abundant life—that is the way Jesus reads the human balance sheet." "Vitality *is* mightier than size," is the way Dr. Fosdick puts it.[2]

Gerald Heard has given us a delightful book that portrays

[1] Pp. 97 ff. New York, Abingdon Press, 1930. Used by permission.
[2] *A Faith for Tough Times*, by Harry Emerson Fosdick, p. 52. New York, Harper and Brothers, 1952. Used by permission.

51

FIRST BAPTIST CHURCH LIBRARY
16TH & "O" STS., N.W.
WASHINGTON, D.C. 20036

the whole evolutionary process by means of a fairy story.[1] Through this unusual medium he points out that the animals that were big, brutal, and overarmed were lost on the way, and the one who clung throughout to sensitivity, general interest, curiosity, and wonder became man, the master of all the beasts. But we in our cities still cling to the illusion that the big, the brutal, the overarmed, and the one equipped with the most gadgets will save civilization.

The superficiality of our urban life is revealed in the newspapers we read, the movies we see, the radio and television programs that are most popular, and in the appeal of the advertisements we confront on every hand. And this superficiality of our cultural life has been standardized throughout the country. Whether in Miami or Chicago or New Orleans or Minneapolis or Omaha or Tulsa or Los Angeles the pattern is the same. Our regional differences, the differences traceable to our national or racial origin, the differences between economic and social levels have been blanketed by a uniform standard that city life epitomizes. Canon Bell thus delineates the American cultural picture: "Ours is a nation of new rich people, well washed, all dressed up, rather pathetically unsure just what it is washed and dressed up for; a nation convinced that a multitude of material goods, standardized, furiously and expensively advertised by appeals to greed and vanity, will in themselves make life worth the living." [2]

This superficiality of city life is in large part explained by the characteristics described in the last two chapters. When

[1] *Gabriel and the Creatures*. New York, Harper and Brothers, 1952.
[2] *Op. cit.*, p. 41. Used by permission.

people move about as they are doing and settle in cities in such vast numbers, the difficulty of digging down beneath the surface of things is increased. Why bother about the people next door and be considerate of them? They will soon be moving, or you may move yourself. So let the radio blast and the children yell. Don't bother your head about the damage to public or private property. You'll soon be off, and someone else can repair it. Irresponsibility comes easily to restless, migratory city dwellers. Why make friends, why seek out churches, why bother about the city government? You will soon be gone—so what's the use?

This philosophy of life is to be found on all levels of city life. The lower classes aspire to the values that the middle and upper classes enjoy. Proletarian culture is distinguishable from bourgeois culture only in degree, not in kind. Cities encourage people to live off the surface of life. They are like water spiders skimpering over the surface of a pond, their movements quick and apparently aimless, guided only by the lure of immediate satisfactions and never exploring the depths of the waters.

. . .   *Beneath the Surface*

And yet there is another side to city life. Nowhere in our American life are there open as many mansions for the spirit of man, so many nourishments for the life of the imagination and the mind. Here are the theaters, the concert halls, the colleges, universities, museums, and adult education centers. Here are intellectual advantages and opportunities that are absent from the small town. Here are the dynamic

53

tensions between people of varied backgrounds, so that, by comparison, life in the small town or country is drab and uninteresting, without stimulus and challenge. So despite its distraction, its rush, its noise, its brashness, its superficiality there are opportunities in the city for a rich and full life of the mind and spirit.

One has only to study the crowds that throng the museums and concert halls of our great cities to realize that it is not just the elite few who appreciate art and music, as Bell seems to think, but a great cross section of the city's population representative of all classes and all national and racial backgrounds. The common man of our cities is not entirely given over to the dominant philosophy of externalism. But he is still far from being a man who understands the meaning of life, a man of moral stature, strength, and resourcefulness of mind and of universal sympathy and friendship and love. And those who would become men of such character have to struggle with a predominating philosophy that keeps men on the surface of life. Our city living polishes the outside of the cup and does not encourage us to peer into the inside of the cup to see what is therein. And this is where the city churches come in.

. . . The Churches—The Outside or the Inside of the Cup?

In the midst of the superficiality of urban life, and ministering to the multitudes whose lives are so often absorbed with the externalities of life, stand our churches. By their very presence in the city they bear witness to the fact that the things that are seen are temporal and the things that are

54

unseen are eternal, that what a man is is much more important than what he has and much more important than what the world thinks he is, that from within come the issues of life—the good and the evil. In the spirit of Him in whose name they minister, the churches are committed to digging down beneath the surface of life to the bedrock of eternal realities upon which life must be built.

Some churches, however, all too accurately reflect the externalism of the city. They measure their effectiveness by the splendor and beauty of their architecture, by the size of the congregation and the rapidity of its growth, by the amount of money raised, by the multiplicity of its activities and organizations, and by the attention given to its program by the press. These are the "great city churches," the "successful churches."

Of the twelve "great churches" intensively studied by *The Christian Century* in 1950, eight were city churches.[1] These ranged in size from 1,800 to 8,000 members. Their average annual budget was $180,000. Their programs of activities were so full and so varied as to require sizeable staffs, one of them having 30 full time employees. Their record of achievement is noteworthy in terms of the redemption of human personalities, the preservation and restoration of family life, in the stimulus given to development of civic virtue, courage, and compassion. Lives have been changed, people helped over the rough spots and led to an understanding of the meaning of life. Christian people have been inspired to share

[1] The reports on these churches, first published in *The Christian Century*, were later brought out in a volume, *Great Churches*; Christian Century Foundation, 1952.

their faith with others, to comprehend and support the world mission of the church, to see the implications of their faith for the social issues of today. Above all, people by the thousands have been brought face to face with God through Jesus Christ, so that they know that life has no meaning and no significance without him.

But it is interesting that the 100,000 Protestant ministers who named the churches to be studied by *The Christian Century* selected from among the city churches eight large and growing congregations, each with a huge budget and an elaborate program of activities. The average city church is a much more modest institution. It has 250 members, a budget of $7,500, and a staff consisting of an inadequately paid minister, a part time sexton, and a part time organist. Could not one church of that type be found that might truly be called great? Are not city folk in these modest churches being redeemed, inspired, brought into the presence of God, and led to walk with him through the distractions and temptations of city life? One fears that even in ecclesiastical and editorial circles greatness is being too often measured by size and growth, financial resources, and multiplicity of activities.

The philosophy of externalism also plays its part in the thinking of people about the church. Any minister can testify to the fact that in his calling the spiritual converse entered into by his people too often begins and ends with the idea of "going to church," as if attendance at services is the chief criterion of one's Christian life, the end of one's Christian endeavor instead of the means to Christian living. There are urban and suburban communities where newcom-

ers are told that "if you want to be somebody here you had
better join the church." Not a few city people take the
position that "it is good business to go to church," or that
the social connections made in church will be valuable to
a matronly social climber or her marriageable daughter.

At the other end of the social scale, there are thousands
of city people who will not go to church nor let their children go to Sunday school because they do not have the
proper clothes. The notion that the church is a respectable
institution for respectable people is hard to down despite the
fact that the church ministers in the name of Him who came
to minister to the lowly and the outcast and was known as
the particular friend of sinners.

A house to house visitation to a large housing project
turned out some interesting conclusions as to why people
preferred one church above the others. The factors determining their decision in the order of their frequency were:
(1) the personality of the minister (he was not necessarily
a man of great preaching ability, but one who seemed
friendly, dynamic, inspiring); (2) the friendliness of the
congregation; (3) the accessibility of the church; (4) the
activities offered; (5) the quality of the music; (6) denominational affiliation. Architecture was never mentioned.

A large part of the success of all the eight city churches
studied by *The Christian Century* was attributed to the
personalities of their ministers. They are all good preachers
but none of them "top-notchers." Some, but not all, have
outstanding executive ability. But all of them are possessed
by a love of people as individuals, a zeal for personal evangelism, and they have maintained a ministry so selflessly

57

devoted that all who have come into contact with them have felt them to be true representatives of the Christ they proclaim, living everything they preach.

. . .   *Within the Cup*

In the life and work of the city pastor and in the program of his church a careful distinction has to be made between ends and means. Architecture, music, a friendly atmosphere, recreational activities, social welfare projects, pastoral counseling, and even services of worship are not ends in themselves. Rather they are means to the end of giving to men and women, boys and girls, a firsthand vivid experience of the presence of God and his Christ in their lives. A confusion of means with ends may make of a city church an architectural museum piece, an esthetic center of culture, a psychiatric clinic, an ecclesiastical Rotary Club, a more or less sanctified recreational center, a beautiful setting for ritual, or a lecture platform. All of this is but the outside of the cup. Look within—what is there? Is God there? And Christ? Is prayer a reality? Is life being well and deeply grounded in the eternal verities? Only when we can answer "yes" to these questions will our city and suburban churches break through the crust of externalism in our urban life and lead city dwellers to build the house of their lives upon a rock, so that come what may, in life or in death, it shall stand.

"Do not be anxious . . ."

How to Conquer Fear," "Why Be Anxious," "How to Get Release from Tension." Such are the sermon topics being announced by an increasing number of city pastors.

Does this reflect just an idiosyncrasy on the part of a few ministers? Is this just a pseudo-psychological hobby that they are riding? Or does it suggest a basic human need of city folk?

Observe the character of the religious books that make the lists of the best-sellers. Note how often one sees titles like these: A *Guide to Confident Living, Peace of Mind, Peace of Soul.*

Study the curriculum of our theological seminaries. Aside from basic courses in theology, Biblical study, and church history, one finds an increasing emphasis on "personal counseling" instead of on "social action" or "religious education," as in an earlier day.

59

These emphases are not just the fads of the moment, but arise out of the felt needs of an increasing number of people who are disturbed, worried, and anxious. In World War II one-fourth of the draftees were rejected as unfit, one half of these because of emotional disturbances. There is a suicide in this country about every half hour. Five hundred thousand of our people are in mental hospitals, and that number would be much larger were there sufficient accommodation available. There are 7 million problem drinkers in this country, of whom 750,000 are chronic alcoholics. Recently, the increase in drug addiction, especially in our cities, has assumed alarming proportions, particularly among teen-age boys and girls.

Seward Hiltner reports in *Pastoral Counseling*,[1] that in one congregation of a hundred members, in the course of a single month the pastor had to deal with the following situations: a boy on parole trying to go straight; another lad on probation; a young woman confused with intellectual doubts; a girl despondent over a broken love affair; a young couple who had just buried their first child; a family in which the mother had just died; a man far advanced in alcoholism; a couple whose marriage was headed for the rocks; another couple worried about their high school youngster; a man facing a serious operation.

We need not be surprised, therefore, to have one of our leading psychotherapists, Rollo May, maintain in *Man's*

[1] P. 15. Nashville, Abingdon-Cokesbury Press, 1949.

Search for Himself [1] that "our age is more anxiety-ridden than any period since the breakdown of the Middle Ages."

. . . *Personality Problems in the City*

It has not been definitely proved that there is a higher rate of personality disintegration in our cities than in the country. It may be that statistics are better kept in the cities or that more cases of mental disturbances find their way to clinics and hospitals in the city than in the country, for psychiatrists and mental health clinics are not readily accessible in rural areas. Nevertheless, if comparable statistics were available, it is highly probable that the city would show a higher percentage of emotional and mental disturbance.

For, as Hallenbeck points out, these characteristics of city life are among those that have been found conducive to mental breakdown: "the isolation of the city person, which lessens his contacts with other people . . . the many impersonal relationships with people who are different in background, education, and even language; . . . the hostility of the city, its controls and its restrictions; the strain of noise, hurry, and insecurity; the inability to deal with the forces which exert determining influences on life." [2]

Psychologists warn us of the danger of insecurity. The city mind is teeming with a sense of both economic and social insecurity. Fear of unemployment, of a dependent old age,

[1] P. 34. New York, W. W. Norton Co., 1953. Used by permission.
[2] *American Urban Communities*, by Wilbur C. Hallenbeck, p. 531. New York, Harper and Brothers, 1953. Used by permission.

61

of sickness or disabling injury with no economic resources, breaks down self-reliance and fills a man with a sense of frustration and futility. He is afraid to take chances or to accept any unnecessary responsibility. He becomes the slave of circumstances, forced to play it safe.

The people of the city are clock minded. The day is begun with an alarm clock and continued by punching a time clock. The lunch hour is measured to the minute. The time for theater and movie going is gauged by the clock. There is little room for spontaneity in the lives of clock minded and schedule minded folk. City people increasingly want to be told what to do and when to do it and how. This is the mood of much of our urbanized life, and it does not make for self-realization and an integrated life.

The other characteristics of city life outlined in the previous chapters would be sufficient to account for the tensions under which city people live. The drive to get ahead so often frustrated and so often misdirected, the setting of people in the midst of a heterogeneous mass of strangers, the constant moving about, the rootless superficiality of city life— such characteristics do not make for well poised, balanced, and integrated personalities.

. . .   *Today's Tensions*

But there are more fundamental causes of our present state of confusion, tension, and anxiety. For forty years we have been subjected to the tensions of wars, both hot and cold. Even now the threat of still another hangs over our heads. Young men see little use in planning the future or pursuing the present constructively with the draft hanging over their heads. Over us all and especially over our cities hangs the threat of atomic warfare with its well publicized potential for total destruction. Why wouldn't we be tense and anxious?

But Dr. May is right in ascribing our present condition to a more fundamental cause that affects all of life but operates in our cities with particular intensity. We are living in one of civilization's transition periods, he maintains; "one way of living is in its death throes and another is being born." For instance, we have been taught to strive to get ahead of the next man. In Chapter I, it was pointed out how large a part that drive plays in city life. But actually "in modern society, characterized by giant business and monopolies and by labor unions, educational and ecclesiastical systems, a man's success depends more on how well one works with one's fellow workers." [1] For many of this generation the old moral and religious sanctions that gave stability to our forefathers no longer seem relevant, and they have not discovered values, objectives, and standards to replace them.

As a result, our life today is characterized by emptiness, loneliness, and anxiety. People do not know what they want, nor do they have a clear idea of what they feel. So their main objective in life is to be accepted by their fellows, to conform, to "fit in." They want to be socially accepted, to be well liked, and are fearful of being alone with themselves.

Authoritarian doctrines such as those of communism

[1] May, *op. cit.*, p. 47. Used by permission.

may rush into the vacuum of modern life to seize possession. Or authoritarian versions of religion may enter to bring a semblance of order. But Christianity can bring into the vacuum an interpretation and plan that will give meaning to life as we confront it today and bring about a new orientation of all man's faculties, convincing him that there are values worth living and dying for.

It is with such considerations in mind that religion must be interpreted to modern city people. Authority and tradition in themselves will not suffice. Religion as a center of inner strength must be revealed again to give city people new courage to be themselves, to stand on their own convictions, to see the truth and live by it.

. . . Spiritual Therapy Needed

To minister to this anxiety ridden generation new insights and means for applying spiritual therapy are clearly called for.

This involves a reconsideration on the part of both minister and people of the function of the church and its clergymen. The need for pastoral counseling is becoming increasingly recognized by the clergy. But the implications of this emphasis have not been fully realized by the members of our congregations. If a minister is to render such service to his people, he must have time and energy to devote to it, and his people must see that he has it.

In most city churches the minister has no staff about him. Only the relatively few large city churches can afford a multiple staff of an assistant minister, secretary, director

64

of religious education, and social worker. The minister is the man of all work. What does the congregation expect of him? Certainly it expects reasonably good sermons requiring time for study and preparation, the visitation of the sick, the enlistment of new members, the direction of the Sunday school and young people's work, the operation of the organizational machinery of the church, and participation in a certain amount of community and ecclesiastical affairs. But too often the pastoral function of the minister has to be neglected for other matters that are pressed upon him. So one who runs about ringing doorbells, passes the time of day regularly with parishioners in hurried calls, and waits upon his people in their sickness and sorrow is called a good pastor.

Parishioners Can Help

But pastoral counseling involves extended and repeated conferences with troubled people. It involves consultation with doctors, psychiatrists, and social workers. Hours can be spent on a single case each week. If this sort of work is to be done, the pastor must be relieved of other time consuming responsibilities. Work with the Sunday school and young people can and should be assumed by the men and women of the church. The operation of the organizational machinery of the church need not be performed by the minister; the laity can and should take care of that. If their pastor has the gift of dealing with the problems of individuals, he should be freed to exercise it, and members of the congregation should realize that there is no more important way for their minister to use his time.

65

In most congregations there are men and women who have the great gift of dealing with people sympathetically and understandingly. They could be of great help to their pastor in handling certain cases of troubled individuals. How many parishioners go to their pastors to inquire whether they can be of help to him in his pastoral counseling? How many ministers have a group of people in their congregations on whose help they can bank in dealing with youngsters in trouble? Is there any reason why there should not be "big brothers" and "big sisters" in each congregation? Happily married couples can speak out of experience to young people whose marriage is headed for the rocks. A physician who is a churchman, a lawyer who has an interest in helping people, a teacher who knows the psychology of growing youngsters can be veritable towers of strength to their minister.

. . .   *Church Clinics*

Of course, if a city church is in a position to organize and maintain a clinic, a ministry of great significance can be carried on.

Quite a few of the larger city churches have organized clinics in which a combined approach of religion and psychiatry is made to the problems of the disturbed, in an effort to prevent disturbances from arising.

One of the churches studied in *The Christian Century* series is known as a "full guidance church." Its pastor states that the church aims "to guide life from birth through all the years of life in the tabernacle of the body." It guides life in the home and through experience beyond the home in the way and the truth that is life eternal and in the love of God that is revealed in Christ. It provides full guidance for the whole family, so that within its house there will be the living church. It helps the person and the family to find the answers upon which all other answers depend, such as: "What is the purpose of life?," "What is the secret of prayer?" The church uses all the resources of the community to build a teamwork for the guidance of its people: psychiatry, psychology, anthropology, sociology, philosophy, arts, and science, all brought to the service of a vital religion for all areas of living.

This program involves premarital counseling, prenatal clinics, child guidance, mental testing, marriage counseling, service to the aged. But all of this is carried on as an integral part of the pastoral program of the church and its evangelistic outreach. Comparatively few churches have the personnel and the resources to carry on as extensive a program as this, though many more could do it if they were so inclined.

. . .   *The Pastoral Ministry*

Every city minister could equip himself for an intelligent and effective use of pastoral counseling and could carry it on without a large paid staff provided his church people would allow him time for such a ministry and would stand by him with personal assistance in meeting the problems he encountered.

Church people should cultivate the habit of turning to their pastor for help in their personal problems. The idea

67

seems to be prevalent that a minister of a city church is too busy for people's problems. The minister who is too busy to have time for people and their troubles is too busy. That is one of the most important aspects of the ministry, and church people should never lose sight of that fact.

I have a letter from a ministerial friend who has devoted his life to the social service aspects of the work of the city church. He has been concerned to make the program of the city church effective in relation to the social needs of its community. Now on retirement he has been serving as interim pastor of a church in a medium sized city. He writes:

My experience here has convinced me that "the cure of souls" is still valid, an open door to needy people everywhere. I am not now thinking of "counseling" and "clinics," which have their place, too, but rather of that old-fashioned intimate sharing of life in the home. It takes a lot of time but it has its great rewards. . . . I had a wedding recently and discovered a few days before that the groom-to-be was a Roman Catholic and he and the bride had agreed not to interfere with each other's religion. I was confronted with the task and opportunity of making clear to both of them what the Christian religion was all about and laying the foundation for a truly Christian home. So I found pastoral work brings up problems of Christian education. . . . A lady called up to arrange for a baptism. Her husband was a Jew, and when the older children had been baptized he had been made to feel very uncomfortable. Could she come alone? I persuaded her to have her husband stand by her, and then I improvised a baptismal service with his sensibilities in mind, but yet, I trust, in keeping with the spirit and attitude of Jesus as he took the children in his arms and blessed them. A day or two later I had a letter from the Jewish father saying, "Both of our families were deeply impressed with the service. Do come to see us." During the summer I had eight funerals—all with attendant pastoral opportunities. Yes, there are rich possibilities in the pastorate in the city even in the summer. They derive from and contribute to the meaning of truly Christian fellowship.

Let us recall the picture of the city man we have drawn: lonely, confused, insecure, empty, anxious. Is there any greater service that can be rendered by a city church, its minister and people, than offering friendship, counsel, and guidance to the multitudes who are as sheep without a shepherd, and who so desperately need a sure foundation upon which to build their lives?

| THE SOCIAL PROBLEMS

OF THE CITY

"Bear one another's burdens . . ."

EVERY one of God's children has a burden to carry. Generally speaking, however, the burdens borne by the average American are lighter than those of the people of any other part of the world. We have not experienced the devastation and destruction of war as have England, many European countries, and latterly, Korea. In our concern about our own social problems, it is well that we keep in mind what has happened to Korea and the Koreans. Of the twenty-one million people in South Korea about one-fourth are homeless, for 600,000 homes have been destroyed. In North Korea it is estimated that bombing and strafing have destroyed 40 per cent of all habitations of any kind. The civilian population of that part of the country has diminished from 9 million to about 4 million—killed in the bombing, dead from malnutrition or cold, fled to the South for freedom, or carried off by the Communist occupiers.

While we have extremes of poverty, few of our citizens have experienced hunger as have millions in India and China. The state of the American Negro gives grave distress to believers in democracy. But compared with the Negroes in parts of Africa, the Negro here lives in a paradise. We have our slums, but at their worst they are preferable to the hovels that millions of people throughout the world call home.

But this is no cause for self-congratulation and complacence. We have the resources of wealth, leadership, and organizational ability to enable us to lift from the shoulders of our citizens many of the most grievous of their burdens. We have made progress. A comparison of the worst slums of our modern cities with those of even a hundred years ago should convince us of that. But the burdens are still there. For our problems have a way of keeping ahead of our solutions. And it is in our cities that the social problems are of the greatest magnitude and the burdens placed upon the common people the heaviest.

Let us hear testimony as to the reality and nature of the burdens that many city people have to bear.

Here speaks the Mayor of one of our large eastern cities:

Decay lies like a dagger at the heart of the city. It is evident in the neighborhoods that grew without plan and fail to satisfy even the basic need for safe and healthy living. It is apparent in the alleys that form an endless network, each harboring its own stories of human misery and deterioration. It is found in the noise and odors of business and industrial enterprises which intrude into areas where people make their homes. And—it is apparent in the hundreds of blocks where hardly a dwelling can be found which offers the standards necessary for decent living.

71

Slums are expensive. Not only do they rob the city of adequate taxes; they also rob the city of the contribution of future citizens who have learned to live without hope or ambition. Furthermore, unchecked blight fans out in all directions, planting in healthy areas the seeds of decay.[1]

A report on a housing survey of 1,000 apartments in another city disclosed the following conditions: 895 families reported rats and rat holes in their apartments; 898 reported broken and loose plaster; 721 families reported defective wiring; 102 families must share a toilet with another family.

The following examples of overcrowding were typical: 3 adults and 10 children in one three-room apartment; 2 adults and 4 children in one room; 6 families in one apartment, sharing one toilet; 17 families using one toilet and one bathroom.

· · ·   *The Major Problems*

The problems of the city most frequently highlighted by sociologists are poverty, disease, delinquency, and housing.

There is poverty in our cities in good times and in bad. For the city man is dependent upon his job, and when that is lost, for whatever reason (depression, accident, sickness, old age, or incompetence), there remains only public relief. The drive to get ahead has brought to the city and kept there the chronic failures, the untrained, and the incompetent, as well as the ambitious, the capable, and the alert.

[1] *Signs of a Better Baltimore.* A joint statement by the Housing Authority of Baltimore City, the Baltimore Redevelopment Commission, and the Baltimore City Health Department.

72

Disease runs rampant where people are crowded together. Sanitation becomes difficult to maintain, contagion difficult to prevent. While the city provides far more adequate hospitals, clinics, and health services than rural areas, these facilities never keep pace with the needs of growing cities. The result is that half of the individuals in the lowest income group receive no medical care whatever.

Delinquency and crime flourish in our cities, offenses involving property being especially common. The breakdown of the home as an economic and social unit and the lack of wholesome recreational facilities have made juvenile delinquency an all too common characteristic of city life. Gangsterism, muggings, holdups, and dope addiction are familiar to teen-agers in the slum areas of our cities.

All these problems tie in with the paramount issue of housing. Wherever people are crowded together in sordid and unhealthy surroundings, we will find a high incidence of poverty, disease, crime, and delinquency.

. . . *Assets and Liabilities in City Districts*

It is possible to plot on a map of any city the sections where the social problems are the gravest and the burdens placed upon the people the heaviest. In general the distribution of the goods and ills of urban life may be plotted according to the following plan, which was used by Samuel C. Kincheloe in his book *The American City and Its Church*.[1]

[1] P. 40. New York, Friendship Press, 1938. Used by permission.

73

I. Downtown Area

Municipal Buildings
Libraries
Museums
Theaters

Big Stores
Office Buildings
Central Banks
Transportation Center

II. Area of Light Industries

Railroad Yards

Wholesale Houses

III. Inner City Area

Foreign Born
  [We can also add Negroes
  and other minority groups]
Poor Housing
Low Rate of Home Ownership
Poor Home Furnishings
Crowding
Poor Light and Air
Poor Play Facilities
No Trees and Grass
Dirty Streets, Alleys
High Birth Rate

High Infant Death Rate
High Death Rate by Tuberculosis
  [And high incidence of
  other diseases]
High Delinquency Rate
Inadequate Food and Clothing
Much Unemployment
High Relief Rates
Low Wages
Outward Movement of Leadership
Concentration of "Ills"

IV. Outer City Area

Mingling of Nationalities
Apartments—High Rent
Low Rate of Home Ownership
Limited Space
Less Smoke and Dirt
Limited Play Facilities
Few Trees—Small Yards

Low Birth Rate
Increasing Delinquency Rate
Adequate Food and Clothing
Medium Relief Rates
Moderate Income
Rapid Movement from Place
  to Place

V. *Residential Suburbs*

Native American	Low Infant Death Rate
Spacious Residences	Low Death Rate by Tubercu-
[Or luxury apartments]	losis
High Rate of Home Owner-	[And low incidence of other
ship	diseases]
Comfortable Furnishings	Low Delinquency Rate
Much Space per Person	Plenty of Food and Clothing
Purer Air	Little Unemployment
Good Play Facilities	Low Relief Rates
Trees and Grass	High Income
Clean Streets	Low Mobility Rate
Low Birth Rate	Concentration of "Goods"

There are, of course, many variations of this distribution plot. In some cities there are many inner city areas and many outer city areas. Cities where heavy industry is concentrated have a different pattern from that of more largely commercial cities and different also from that of cities where recreation is the center of life (*e.g.* Miami) or where education and culture provide the hub for the city's revolving life (*e.g.* Ann Arbor, Berkeley, New Haven). And there are some cities that are purely residential, with no inner city within their bounds, although most of them are satellite cities, with the inner city and its problems concentrated in a municipality twenty-five or even fifty miles distant, within commuting distance.

But wherever there are low income groups, there you will find a piling up of the social problems of the city, for the basic problems of urban society are interrelated. This is not to say that the city people whose lives are solidly grounded economically do not have their problems. If that were so, the Kingdom would be near at hand in our better residential

75

and suburban areas. People who have plenty of money have their burdens to carry, and people with too much money have many ways of getting into trouble. Not the least of these problems are those of self-satisfaction, complacency, and the lack of concern for the welfare of less fortunate fellow citizens. And this is where the Christian churches of our cities have an important role to play.

. . . *Burdens Common to All*

The burdens that city people have to carry may be divided into two groups: (1) the burdens that concern the internalities of life and (2) those having to do with the external aspects of life. The first set of problems concerns all city people alike. Death, sorrow, pain, suffering, and illness come to all men, and the church is concerned with how individuals face these inevitabilities of life. The problems discussed in previous chapters, the drive to get ahead, secularism, materialism, loneliness, friendlessness, mobility, rootlessness, superficiality, the moral sag, tension, anxiety, fear, the breakdown of the home and the marriage tie are common to all city people of whatever class and area. To these problems every church must address itself, for the church is the bearer of good news to distressed and needy individuals.

. . . *The Special Burdens of the Poor*

Other burdens are placed upon individuals and groups from without by the nature of our urban social order, and it is with these that we are primarily concerned in this chapter.

As will be noted in the description of the distribution of social goods and ills in the city, there is a concentration of social problems in the inner city. However, despite the congestion that exists in the inner city, most city people live in the outer city areas, in the residential sections of the city or in the suburbs. It is also true that most Protestant churches are located in these relatively favorable areas for reasons (good and bad) that we shall discuss later.

Accordingly, one of the great questions confronting the Protestant churches of our cities is the part to be played by them in lifting from the backs of our less favored fellow citizens the burdens imposed upon them from without.

. . . *Churches as Burden Lifters*

The churches have a clear responsibility for the development in their members of a sense of civic responsibility. Our municipal governments are notoriously inefficient and corrupt. One reason for this almost universal condition is that the so-called decent citizens take such an insignificant part in city politics and city government. Only periodically, when a "reform movement" gathers momentum, do most Protestant churches and church people pay any attention to the problems of city government.

Local churches can do much to foster an intelligent, conscientious, dynamic public opinion. Former Governor Youngdahl of Minnesota testifies that it was the support of the churches that made possible the initiation and maintenance of his program of humane and curative treatment of the mentally ill, of youth conservation, and of the protection

77

of the people from the rapacity and corruption of organized gambling. It is in a large measure due to the support of the churches that the vice element has been driven from Minneapolis and the rule of the mob broken.

On the other hand, in a recent study by the World Council of Churches of the evangelistic and social service activities of the Protestant churches of Kansas City, Missouri, it is stated:

No instances were discovered where church bodies had joined in action to improve the civic and community morale by the elimination of undesirable activities in Kansas City, such as the sale of obscene literature on newsstands. Nor was any positive action noted to participate in or give leadership to political activities of any character. When the crime situation was before the public in large headlines, sermons were preached dealing with the subject, but there issued no group action expressive of church membership indignation.

The all too familiar pattern of city churches is to move out into or locate in the favored residential areas of the city and to ignore entirely the social problems that they have left behind and know only from a distance. They show little concern for lifting the burdens of their fellow citizens that have an indirect influence upon their own lives.

. . .   *Rallying behind Front Line Churches*

In addition to arousing public opinion, churches in a favored area have a responsibility to rally support for those who are sacrificially endeavoring to deal with the social problems of the city at first hand and through the church.

78

In almost every city there are churches or church supported institutions that are facing the worst problems of the city with courage, vision, and self-dedication. Not all Protestant churches have fled when population changes transformed their neighborhoods from pleasant residential districts into areas of physical and moral deterioration. Despite the fact that few middle class Protestant people are available, and these are surrounded by a vast multitude whose varied national, racial, economic, and social backgrounds give rise to staggering human needs, they have stood their ground. Bad housing, with its concomitant problems of health, delinquency, and crime; the prevalence of low incomes, which takes the "labor problem" out of the realm of the academic into the cruel realities of the struggle for existence; the intermingling of nationalities and races, testing every day the validity of the democracy and brotherhood we profess—these are the problems confronted by the relatively few churches and church supported institutions ministering to the inner city.

Most of the Protestant people in our pews are entirely unaware of the heroic battle being waged by the churches and church institutions in the inner city. They are unacquainted with the problems and needs of slum areas in the city and not much effort is made to let them know what is going on. Denominational headquarters have been concerned, and rightly, with the churching of the new residential areas springing up around so many of our cities. This emphasis is needed, for the people moving into these rapidly growing suburbs need the gospel as desperately as any other group. It must not be forgotten, however, that if suburbanites really absorb the gospel it will result in a growing concern on their part for the underprivileged areas of the city. No city nor suburban church can rightly be called a successful institution unless its people are concerned with the broader problems of city life and are led to cultivate an intelligent interest in the areas where the other half lives. It is encouraging that denominational leaders are realizing that, along with church extension, an intensification of the program of the church in the inner city must take place.

Significant and imaginative approaches are being made to the problems of the inner city. One church made a demonstration of what can be done in slum rehabilitation by purchasing a broken down house, renovating it with its own labor and at its own expense, and presenting it to the city as a demonstration of what can be done by other owners of deteriorated property. A church group organized its own members to make a housing survey to discover the extent of housing violations and stimulate the enforcement of city housing laws. Churches in transition neighborhoods have transformed themselves into inclusive churches where Negroes and whites may worship side by side. Other churches have established close and friendly cooperative relationships with organized labor. Church supported institutions are demonstrating that youngsters living in slum areas need not be juvenile delinquents who graduate to a life of crime. Many churches are carrying on a hand to hand battle with alcoholism, drug addiction, and sexual promiscuity. To them, broken homes, sordid living, economic insecurity, unemployment, street gangs fighting with one another and organized depredations against law and order, are matters of everyday concern and firsthand experience. Churches are waging battles for social justice, battles fought with the people and for the people. In some places, they are patiently and lovingly carrying on "ambulance work" to meet the appalling crises of daily living.

All of this will be documented in later chapters. At this point it is sufficient to make clear that there are churches, church leaders, and church institutions that are manfully endeavoring to lift the burdens of life from the shoulders of those city people who are most apt to be bowed down by them. There are not enough such churches and church leaders, and they receive too little support. Yet these are the churches that occupy the front lines in the battle against the ills of the city. These have the right to be recognized as "the great city churches," "the successful churches."

part two | GOD IN THE CITY

"Go therefore and make disciples . . ."

I AM always interested in church bulletin boards and in announcements of sermon topics appearing in our city newspapers. Frankly, most of them do not say much that would attract the attention of intelligent readers or even provoke a second thought.

But not long ago I saw a sign outside a church that stopped me in my tracks. It read: *"This Church Exists for the Sake of Those Outside of It."* "Is that really true?" I asked myself. Of course, it is not a completely true statement of the function of the local church. Each church still has some work to do on the people inside of it. They are not necessarily ready to be fitted for their angels' wings just because they are in the church. And, looking ahead, we see the certainty that most of their children will grow up to be spiritual illiterates unless the church does some work with them.

But the local church does have a mission to those outside. One reason why a church has a minister, a building, and a membership is that witness to the dynamic power of the gospel may be borne to those outside of it. A church does not simply *have* a missionary society; it *is* a missionary society. It not only believes in evangelism and supports it elsewhere; it is an evangelizing agency right where it is. Else it has no warrant to bear the name "Christian."

In our American cities those outside the church (any church) are about as numerous as those inside.

A few years ago I wrote an article bearing the title "City of Wistful Pagans." It received quite a little attention—not all favorable, by any means. Some newspapers felt that I was besmirching the name of my fair city by implying that its people were pagans. Of course, pagans are not necessarily people of bad morals. Some of my best friends are pagans. Some of our highest civilizations have been essentially pagan. What is implied by the term is that to multitudes of our city folk religious faith is not central nor controlling.

That does not mean that many city people will classify themselves as irreligious. In almost every survey made of city churches, it is discovered that the number of people who will identify themselves as of "no faith" is infinitesimally small. Practically everyone will say "I am a Protestant," or "I am a Catholic," or "I am a Jew." But survey after survey reveals a great discrepancy between the statistics bearing on "religious background" and the statistics that are based on the records of the three faiths as to "active membership" or "active participation." Here are excerpts from reports of surveys made in widely scattered cities:

Wilmington, Delaware: "One half of the population is unaccounted for on the rolls of the churches."

Seattle, Washington: "At most, 29 per cent of the total population can be accounted for as members of churches or religious organizations."

San Diego, California: "Only 27.6 per cent of the population are members of any church. And 4 out of 5 of San Diegans are favorable to the Protestant viewpoint."

Hartford, Connecticut: "The total population of the Protestant churches is less than half the population of Protestant antecedents."

Indianapolis, Indiana: "Up to 50 per cent of the population has no vital nor significant relationship to any local religious organization."

New York City: "The religious background of the people of the city can be thus classified: Roman Catholic, 50 per cent; Jewish, 30 per cent; Protestant, 20 per cent." But those claimed as active adherents by the three faiths (and claims as to church affiliation are never modest) total only 50 per cent of the population.

Greater Washington, D. C., reports Protestant church membership, 370,000; Roman Catholic, 120,000; Jewish, 45,000; and *unaffiliated* and largely nominally Protestant, 876,700.

Paducah, Kentucky: It was reported in the first religious survey that of the itinerant workers living in the trailer camps about the nearby defense plant "90 per cent have no church connection."

Of the Chinese population in the United States, only 10 per cent are Christians.

Statistics would vary greatly from city to city and from section to section. Church affiliation and church attendance in the South and Southwest and to a lesser extent in the

Middle West would be higher than in the New England, Middle Atlantic, and Pacific Coast states. Suburban communities would make a better showing than the cities themselves. Churches in residential parts of the city with a relatively stable, home owning population would reach more of their people than the areas where apartment houses, tenements, flats, or boarding houses predominate. The factors making for a higher degree of church affiliation are economic stability, community homogeneity, and those indefinite but real factors involved in the mores of the city or section of the country. In Atlanta or in Orlando, Florida, the thing to do every Sunday is to go to church. In New York to go to church is "the thing to do" only on Easter Sunday. There are city neighborhoods where less than 5 per cent of the people on a block will find their way to a church on a given Sunday.

The city is not more pagan than the rural districts. Quite the contrary. And city churches tend to be larger, better financed and housed, and more highly organized. This leads one observer to assert that "it is not true that the city is the abode of godlessness." Visitors from abroad are impressed with the size of our city churches and their apparent influence upon the life of their members, as compared with conditions they have observed in England or France or the Scandinavian countries.

But it still remains true that a large proportion of our city people are either irresponsive to the appeal of the church or neglected by the church. And since our cities so largely shape the moral climate of the country and set our standards of behavior and values, we are perfectly justified in thinking

86

of the city as one of the greatest mission fields of the Protestant churches.

. . .   *Who Are the Unchurched?*

Who are these unreached, unchurched people, and how did they get that way? Generalizations are dangerous. For in this group are people of all kinds and conditions: folk of immigrant background and Mayflower descendants, white people and non-white, rich and poor and middle-income folk, educated and uneducated, white collar workers, skilled and unskilled labor, financiers, industrialists, executives and their employees, the unemployed and unemployable. All of them are subject more or less to the influences of modern urban life described in the previous chapters: the drive to get ahead, the anonymity and loneliness of the city, the current restless moving about, the superficiality and rootlessness of city life, the tensions, the gigantic social and economic problems. But some groups among the unreached may be singled out and identified.

. . .   *The Intellectuals*

First, the intellectuals are strongly represented among those outside of the church. Let anyone check the list of his friends who are graduates of large universities and colleges and he will find that a large proportion go to church only for a wedding, a funeral, or an Easter Sunday service. What is more serious, a large section of our intellectuals, while giving lip service to the necessity of some sort of re-

87

ligious faith, have no conception of the implications of that faith for daily living and no inclination to put it into action.

Many of the teachers of our youth have a scarcely concealed disdain for the church, its message, and its program. We are now reaping the fruits of building a public educational system that has no place in it for religion; many of our best educated people attach the same importance to religion as do the schools which is none at all.

. . . *Labor*

A second group widely represented among those outside the church is organized labor. This is a numerous, self-conscious, and powerful group. It is true that there are many more members of labor unions in our church membership than is generally supposed. The Protestant churches of Detroit, for example, are filled with men off the assembly lines of the automobile factories. But this group has scanty representation on the official boards of local churches or on the denominational boards. Consequently, we need not be surprised that, rightly or wrongly, the rank and file of organized labor has the impression that the Protestant church is a middle class and upper class institution with little or no interest in the struggles and aspirations of labor.

. . . *The Depressed Groups*

In the third place, the depressed groups in our cities—the economically disenfranchised, the social "outcasts," the members of our various minority groups, are heavily repre-

88

sented in the unchurched group. Negroes, for example, are not "incurably religious." A very large percentage of them are not touched at all by the multitudinous churches that minister to them. Mexicans in the Southwest, Puerto Ricans in our Northern cities stay away from their ancestral Roman Catholic Church in droves. The people on relief, the masses who are crowded into the tenements in our larger cities, and the people who live "on the other side of the tracks" in our smaller cities seem to feel that the churches have no interest in them and no program to meet their needs.

Passive Pagans

Then there is a large group, composed of people of all classes and conditions, who might be called passive pagans. They will say that they believe in God; they do not oppose the church; they just stay away from it and plan their lives without any reference to religion. They have adopted completely, consciously or unconsciously, the secularistic philosophy of life. Their outlook on life is limited to this world only and has no meaning beyond the immediate experience of life's events. With most people this philosophy is not consciously formulated or expressed, but issues in unreflective indifference to religious values.

How Fares Protestantism in America?

In considering the missionary task of the churches in our cities it is necessary to bear in mind other factors than the statistical evidence as to those outside the church and an analysis of the composition of the unchurched group. Charles Clayton Morrison in his book *Can Protestantism Win America?* rightly points out that "the problem of measuring the strength of Protestantism is threefold: First, it is quantitative: Is Protestantism growing in numbers? Second, it is qualitative: Is Protestantism growing stronger in its interior life—in spiritual depth, in an intelligent grasp of its faith, in the bonds which make for its solidarity? And third, it is relative: Is Protestantism advancing in relation to the other forces which are competing for ascendancy in American culture?" [1]

Quantitatively Protestantism is gaining, even in our cities, although in some of them it is losing out badly.

But as to the qualitative measurement, Morrison has grave doubts, and he asks such searching questions as these: "How seriously do the members of Protestant churches regard their membership? How deep going are the commitments which the church evokes in the life of its members and in its appeal for new members? How intelligent is the membership with respect to the meaning of the Christian faith? How firm is the bond of loyalty that holds the members together? How conscious are the local church and the denomination of their organic relation to the whole of Protestantism?" [2]

Just to raise such questions is to set us wondering whether all the pagans are to be found outside the church or whether an important part of our missionary task in the city should not be to deepen the Christian life of those already inside.

[1] P. 6. New York, Harper and Brothers, 1948. Used by permission.
[2] *Ibid.*, p. 5. Used by permission.

As to the status of Protestantism *vis-à-vis* Catholicism and secularism, Morrison believes that both these forces are currently outdistancing Protestantism in their bids for ascendancy in our cultural life.

So the churches of our cities confront a missionary task of huge dimensions and of many ramifications.

. . .   *Wistful Pagans*

And yet we must realize, too, that in approaching our task we shall be dealing with many people who are not at all happy in the prevailing secularistic faith described above. City people are restless, disillusioned, wistful. Many are discovering that political and economic problems can only be solved on a moral basis. They are becoming skeptical of the satisfactions of materialism. They feel lost in the mob, lost in their jobs, lost in a society that seems to grow ever more impersonal and indifferent. They hunger for the experience of a personal faith.

The modern city man may be a pagan, but he is a wistful pagan. Our cities are full of such people, madly pursuing materialistic ends but satisfied neither with the pursuit nor the attainment; searching for something higher and better to live for and to live by; yearning for something more satisfying than mere shelter, food, clothes, and entertainment; unconsciously wanting to live a life, not just make a living.

We are not dealing with a dead weight of negative indifferentism. There is a ferment among the masses of city people that makes the task of reaching the unreached not so much an unsoluble problem as a magnificent opportunity.

A newspaper reporter recently recorded in a book the impressions gathered on a tour throughout this country, made for the express purpose of discovering whether the American people are showing signs of a "return to religion." [1] His observations convinced him that "Americans elsewhere are turning to God as they never have before. Some . . . want to throw in the chips and let God take over. Some just want God to pull their chestnuts out of the fire. Some, badly frightened, are rushing to the security of God's apron string. Some sincerely want to find God and abide with him." [2]

The popularity of religious books is another sign of the times. Thousands outside the churches have been reading the books of Thomas Merton, Norman Vincent Peale, Lloyd Douglas, and Peter Marshall. The popularity of religious programs on the radio and on television is due in a large measure to the fact that they make an appeal to many wistful folk outside the church who want to discover the meaning of life and to gain power to live it on a higher level.

. . . *Needed: An Aggressive Outreach*

The church must go out after the people who are outside the church. We cannot sit back and wait for them to come to us. Too many people in the city say to a church caller: "I have lived in this city for fifteen years, and this is the first

---

[1] *A Reporter in Search of God*, by Howard Whitman. New York, Doubleday and Co., 1953. Used by permission.
[2] *Ibid.*, p. 14. Used by permission.

time any minister ever called on us." City pastors are too
often overburdened with organizational matters. They are
the chore boys of the church and the community. They must
make it clear that one of the most important parts of the
Lord's business is to get out after people in their homes, in
their offices, in their factories. In most cases, a large part of
this visitation evangelism can be done by the laity. The testimony of a church member as to what his faith means to
him is the most effective means possible of reaching the unreached.

The Methodist Church has lately been conducting a
nationwide advance program of evangelism. The reports
are encouraging. In Cleveland, Ohio, the 49 Methodist
churches enlisted 1,500 men and women in a canvass of the
city. It resulted in 2,580 new members. In Columbus, Ohio,
the result of a canvass was 2,503 new members; in Cam-
bridge, Ohio, 1,210; in Portsmouth, Ohio, 1,068; and in
Memphis, Tennessee, 5,617.

Some churches confronting new housing projects have
carried on a systematic canvass that resulted in uncovering
several hundred families who were prospects for church
membership. In Chapter III, reference was made to the
work being carried on in the new defense projects at Savannah River, Paducah, and in the Scioto Valley of Ohio, where
the churches have sent in workers to live in a trailer in the
midst of the huge trailer camps. In older cities, too, the
church must have ministers and members who live where
the people live and can shape and interpret the message and
program of the church in terms of the conditions of their
daily life.

The phenomenal growth of the Pentecostal churches and similar groups in our cities is due in no small measure to the fact that the members are testifying to their faith in season and out of season. If our faith means much to us, we must share it, and the place to begin is in our own community and among all the people who are found there.

. . . *Needed: More Friendliness*

If we are to hold the people who are brought within the doors of our church, the church must be a friendly place for all kinds of people. Too many people report that when they go to a church as strangers no one ever greets them except the pastor at the door. This is especially true of people who are not "our kind." Many a wistful visitor with a "foreign" look or calloused hands or a black face who has gone into a church seeking fellowship has come away feeling that he is just not wanted in that church.

It takes courage, patience, and sometimes a long educational process to make a local church truly inclusive and genuinely friendly. But it can be done. It is being done, as we shall see.

. . . *Needed: Intellectual Alertness*

Again, and this is particularly pertinent in trying to reach the intellectuals and the culturally elite, the church must readjust its program so as to avoid the impression of dullness and stodginess. The careless order of service, the boresome offerings of the choir, the deadly ministerial voice, the mes-

94

sages that are completely irrelevant to the issues of the day —all these must go if the church wishes to interest those who are intellectually alert and culturally literate. Possibly one secret of the success of the late Peter Marshall, whose preaching was as effective as it was popular, was that he threw away all the conventional ideas as to the form and delivery of the sermon and dared to be his original, irrepressible, winsome self.

. . .   *Needed: A Program at Grips with Life*

Again, the church must come to grip with the problems of the people it would serve. This does not mean that the pulpit should concern itself exclusively or even predominately with current issues. But there are many ways in which the church can make it clear that it occupies no ivory tower. There are community problems that the church members must face as Christians. There are social problems that bear down heavily on the life of the city. There is race prejudice rampant in many a city. It is not enough that our denominations and our National Council deliver themselves of resolutions in regard to church and state, the race problem, the economic system, and our housing needs. These resolutions need to be studied and implemented in our local churches.

In the difficult areas of the city a church standing in the midst of stark human need must shape its program to meet those needs in a realistic way. It is by so doing that the church bears the most effective witness to the relevance of its gospel.

95

. . . *"Don't Fence Me In"*

In defining the outreach of a local church there is a good directive in the title of the popular song "Don't Fence Me In." Let us not be fenced in by denominationalism and seek out only those who have in the past belonged to our particular branch of the church. To the unchurched elements of the city, denominational affiliation has little or no meaning. As has been said many times in this book, a local church cannot fence itself in so as to exclude people of different racial, national, educational, social, or economic background. For a Christian church, all God's children are "our kind of people." Furthermore, let us not confine ourselves in our outreach to "the Protestant potential." Here I take issue with many of our professional surveyors of city churches. They measure the potential ministry of a local church by the number of people of Protestant background. But what of those of Catholic background or Jewish background who are not actively connected or interested in their ancestral faith and who, along with backsliding Protestants, help to make up the unchurched population of our cities and create the secularistic paganism of our urban life? Have our Protestant churches no mission, no message to them?

There are churches in our cities whose membership has been drawn almost entirely from such groups—Italians, Russians, Czechs, Puerto Ricans, Mexicans, and Jews. There are sections in our cities where these form practically the only constituency available to a Protestant church. Should such a church close because there is no "Protestant potential"? God forbid that a church should be closed for this reason.

Let us not be afraid of being accused of proselyting. The Roman Catholic Church feels free to launch an aggressive missionary program among the mountain people of the South and the Negroes of our Northern cities and succeeds in winning many whom we Protestants have failed to hold. Why, then, should we feel estopped from ministering to those who once were Roman Catholics or whose parents were Catholic, but who presently have no active interest in the old church? The whole city is our field, and all the people in it who do not have a vital connection with another religious body make up our "Protestant potential."

To sum up: If we are to reach the wistful pagans of our cities with a vital faith, the complacent, self-satisfied, stereotyped, stodgy, inward looking, intellectually sterile, socially fearful, one class church must give way to a live, imaginative, restless, outward looking, socially adventuresome, intellectually alert, inclusive church, ready to meet all the needs of all the people of the community in the name and in the spirit of Christ. Only thus will the city church have a chance to win the allegiance of those presently outside it.

eight | THE CHURCH IN THE
INNER CITY

"To preach the gospel to the poor"

SIMEON STYLITES, the popular columnist of *The Christian Century*, opened one of his articles in the following manner:

A big deep voice boomed out in the aisle of the pullman, "How do you like Kansas City?" The little man in the corner looked out of the car window at all of the city that was in view— part of a flight of stairs, a few feet of concrete platform, and two trash cans. "It's an awful dump," he announced.

That is what is technically called "generalizing on insufficient data." The dogmatist who gave the verdict that Kansas City was a dump did not see the city—its parks, its boulevards, its homes, its buildings, and the beautiful station itself. He had only a worm's-eye view.[1]

This worm's-eye view is all that a visitor to Kansas City or any other large American city would have if he traveled through the inner city. For viewing the slums, with their un-

[1] *The Christian Century*, April 15, 1953, p. 442. Used by permission.

collected garbage strewn over the sidewalks and vacant lots, with their dirty streets and crowded tenement buildings, any visitor would say "This city is an awful dump."

. . . *What Is the "Inner City"?*

What is "the inner city"? Where do you find it and what is it like?

To tell the truth, most visitors to our cities know nothing of such a section. The theater district, the shopping center, the financial and business section, and the best residential areas—these are well known. But the inner city is a section that most people pass through by train or bus or car and never really see. It is the city's backyard and most cities are not proud of it; nor have they reason to be.

For "the inner city" is the name widely used to indicate the area of the city that has the greatest accumulation of social needs. The term has come into common usage as a result of the studies made of the social structure of our American cities. The growth of our larger cities and the development of the economic and social life of its people reveal the pattern of a concentric circle, and near the center is the inner city.

The city of Chicago, for example, centers about the Loop, with its concentration of office buildings, large stores, hotels, and theaters. Next to it is a slum area, decidedly in transition, but characterized by the older "foreign" settlements, a Chinatown, a vice area, a skid row, and the beginning of a black belt. Further out is a zone characterized by working-men's homes, largely of older immigrant groups, a two flat

99

section, and the continuation of the black belt. Beyond that, one finds apartment houses, residential hotels, and, finally, single family dwellings. Still further out is a bungalow section, and beyond that lies suburbia, the commuters' paradise.

In Chicago, the inner city is clearly defined as comprising the two zones immediately adjacent to the Loop. Similarly, Detroit has a rather clear demarcation of its inner city in the area bounded by the semicircular Grand Boulevard. Studies of Albany, New York; Cincinnati, Indianapolis, Los Angeles, Minneapolis, Philadelphia, Pittsburgh, and Rochester, New York; St. Louis and Springfield, Massachusetts; Washington, D. C., and Wichita, Kansas, reveal substantially the same pattern. There is a geographically identifiable area near the center of the city that is characterized by poverty, congestion, poor housing, high rates of dependency, delinquency, and infant mortality. Often, the people who live there are newcomers to the city, Negroes, Mexicans, or Puerto Ricans; the residue of the older immigrant groups, Italians, Poles, etc.; or those from the rural and mountain areas of the country who have been lured to the city by the relatively high wages of industry.

To be sure, the phrase "inner city" does not fit into the geography of all cities. In some cities the sort of area described is on the outskirts, or "across the tracks," or "out by the steel plant," or "close by the mill." The largest cities have more than one slum area, and none of them are near the center of the city. In the Borough of Manhattan (New York City) there are at least six areas that show a high concentration of social needs and none of them is near the center of the city, and the four other boroughs of the city would reveal many more such needy areas.

Centers of Human Need

We are not dealing so much with geography as with human need. And there are few cities in this country, if any, that do not have their "pockets" where the poor and needy live. Here is a suburban city of some 15,000 people. It gives every appearance of prosperity, middle class comfort, and some wealth. There is a small group of Negroes, most of whom are now prospering. But in a section of two or three blocks, the poorest Negroes live in dilapidated shacks, and out of these few blocks come most of that city's cases of dependency, delinquency, and poor health.

If the people of any city are tempted to say "we have no slums here," let them go to the city's records of relief cases, juvenile delinquency, and infant mortality, and undoubtedly they will find a concentration of such cases in a given area, even if it comprises only a few blocks.

For our purposes, then, the inner city is that area of the city where the poor and needy live, no matter what its geographical location.

The Church and the Inner City

These are the areas that present to the Protestant churches their major missionary task and opportunity. And it is in such areas that our Protestant churches have failed and are failing most lamentably.

The behavior of our churches in the face of deterioration of city neighborhoods has been to retreat. As inner city areas have developed, the Protestant churches have fled to the more desirable sections of the city. We have acted as if the Protestant churches have a mission only to the middle and upper class brackets, composed of people of the Nordic strains and of Protestant backgrounds. Where churches have remained, they have too often stayed to minister to the faithful few who come back to the old church out of sentiment and to the dwindling middle class Protestant remnant to be found in the old neighborhood. We have acted as if it were true that the Protestant churches are creatures of their environment and can only operate successfully when that environment produces a stable population of white middle class people of Protestant antecedents. We conform to the urban world instead of endeavoring to transform it.

We Protestants are concentrating much of our attention and resources upon the task of churching new residential areas. But what of the older sections of the city? Must they be neglected and their people abandoned to the forces of irreligion? Must they look only to store front churches conducted by the more emotional sects to give to them the moral and spiritual undergirding so vitally necessary in areas where the strain and stress of city life press most heavily and disastrously upon individual character and group life?

We may be thankful that some local churches and some Protestant missionary agencies have realized the magnitude of the opportunity presented in the inner city and are addressing themselves to it with vision and vigor. The projects described below are selected with a view to illustrating some of the emphases and attitudes that are essential in a ministry to the inner city area.

. . . *Essentials of a Missionary Program*

1. A SENSE OF MISSION

In a typical inner city area of Chicago, there is a Lutheran church that was started seventy-five years ago to minister to the German and Scandinavian immigrants of that persuasion. A handsome edifice was erected and a program developed that was outstanding in effectiveness and influence. Then, soon after the turn of the century, came the deluge. Newly arrived Jewish and Polish immigrants inundated the area, and the German and Scandinavian constituents of the church moved out. The church was tempted to move after them. The Synod urged such a step. Thirty other Protestant churches in the area folded their tents and silently stole away to more favorable areas. But the pastor, backed by some of his leading members, took the stand that this church had a mission to "serve its community rather than its constituency," and the church stood its ground.

Today the area does not give the appearance of deterioration. On the contrary, it seems like a neighborhood of substantial, well built homes. But a visit inside some of them is sufficient to make one wonder how landlords can stretch their consciences sufficiently to charge any rents at all, let alone the exorbitant sums they do charge. And crowded into these old homes are people of many nationalities and faiths, Jewish, Orthodox, and Catholic, with Negro and Puerto Rican families beginning to move in and with over a thousand Russian and Polish displaced persons coming to make their first American homes there. It is an area with a high rate of sickness, illiteracy, delinquency, and relief cases.

Here the church offers a seven day a week program. It has its church services and religious education program, centering about its beautiful sanctuary. It also has a fullfledged recreational program for the children of the community, a counseling service that is particularly valuable to the newly arrived DP's, and a ministry to alcoholics. It operates a mobile chapel with a sound truck for street preaching and the showing of motion pictures. The work is supported by the old members of the congregation and the denominational mission board. It is a courageous effort to demonstrate that a large city church has a continuing mission in a radically changed environment.

2. SERVING MINORITY GROUPS

This sense of mission for the poorer areas of our cities is reflected in the foreign language churches that have been organized by the various denominations for the most part in inner city areas. This work among Italian, Magyar, Polish, and Czech immigrants, and more recently, among the Mexicans and Puerto Ricans, represents a fine concern on the part of the Protestant group for the spiritual welfare of these new arrivals. There is presently a disposition on the part of Protestant church leaders to discount the value of this phase of city missionary work, because there seems to be little to show for it in terms of self supporting churches of continuing usefulness. There is, of course, no permanent place for a foreign language church in this country. But Dr.

William P. Shriver, one of the pioneers in city church work, is quite right in his conviction that the missionary adventure, begun in a ministry to immigrant groups in their own language, is not over. Writing of the work among Italians, Dr. Shriver says:

The Italian immigrants and their descendants have made astonishing progress. They are destined to play an increasing part in our forming American life. . . . Yet great numbers of them are as religiously illiterate today as when the work was started with such enthusiasm sixty years ago. I continue to covet for them Christian enlightenment, freedom for discovery, and the creative fellowship of a truly Christian church—great gifts of evangelical Christianity.[1]

The work carried on over these many years among the immigrant groups must now be assumed by regular American churches, for the foreign language is no longer necessary. The foreign language churches have sown seed that other churches can bring to a rich harvest if they will, for the children and grandchildren of the immigrants are now to be found in the better residential areas and under the very eaves of many of our old-line American churches.

Into the inner city there have moved Mexicans, Puerto Ricans, Negroes, and transient whites from our rural and mountain areas. The same sense of mission that a generation ago led us to endeavor to meet the needs of earlier groups must lead us now to a ministry to the more recent newcomers. Churches and church supported Neighborhood Houses and Homes of Friendly Service must adapt their

---

[1] *Adventure in Missions*, by William P. Shriver, pp. ix ff. The Board of National Missions of the Presbyterian Church in the U. S. A., 1946. Used by permission.

programs to changing conditions and a different population. New ways of ministering must be sought and found. Above all, there must be awakened within us a sense that the church has a mission to the people living in the inner city areas.

A study made in 1953 of Protestant work among the Puerto Ricans in New York City revealed that few of the old-line Protestant churches established in communities into which Puerto Ricans are moving have made an attempt to minister to their new neighbors.

The same study discovered no less than 181 Spanish-speaking Protestant churches in New York City. Of this total, over half are Pentecostal. Most of these are small churches, but the report says of them:

They are indigenous and dynamic. They are self starting and self supporting. They are evangelical and missionary minded. They have a high ratio of lay leadership and responsibility. Tithing is a common practice. So it is not uncommon for churches of one hundred members or less to support a full time pastor and part time missionary and to contribute substantially to missionary work elsewhere.[1]

The Protestant churches can no longer airily dismiss the Pentecostal groups as "emotional sects." We can all learn much from them as to missionary zeal, their sense of stewardship, and their development of a genuine fellowship of committed Christians.

The response to such a ministry is its own reward. Thus a missionary in a Chinese Baptist church in San Francisco

[1] *Mid-Century Pioneers and Protestants*; Meryl H. Ruoss, survey director. Pathfinding Service for the Churches, 105 East 22nd St., New York, N. Y.

writes: "Christianity is a way of life, and demands, out of a heart overflowing with love and gratitude, the entire life of a person. The evidence of a true religion is when one reaches out hungrily to his fellow men."

3. AN INCLUSIVE SPIRIT

The ministry of the church in the inner city area cannot be fenced in, restricted to one group of people and excluding others. Inclusiveness is particularly pertinent in cities where the Negro population is increasing so rapidly that many a Protestant church that hitherto has had an exclusively white constituency is finding Negroes at its very doors.

The familiar behavior pattern has been for such a church to hang on to its segregated constituency as long as possible, then sell out to a Negro church and move out to a new white neighborhood. However, inner city churches in encouraging numbers are seeking and finding a different kind of solution.

For example, a church located in the inner city of Detroit faced this situation: Between 1940 and 1950 the total population of the census tract in which the church is located actually decreased, but the Negro population increased from 2,905 to 18,819. The pastor and his officers faced the following alternatives: (1) to relocate the church, (2) to stay but confine its ministry to the white people in the neighborhood, or (3) to try to create a fellowship of all believers.

The first alternative was rejected because nearly half of the present membership still live in the neighborhood and the outlying areas of the city already have plenty of churches, the second because an artificial restriction of membership would be contrary to the Christian gospel. The reasons advanced for the creation of a fellowship of all believers were: (1) democracy's handling of the color problem has world wide significance; (2) the church has repeatedly declared its belief in a nonsegregated church in a nonsegregated society, and it is time it practiced what it has been preaching; (3) the Christian church should lead other groups in breaking down the undemocratic pattern of discrimination and segregation. Actually, the church in this respect trails the arts, with Marion Anderson; the sciences, with George Washington Carver; the theater, with Ethel Waters; sports, with Jackie Robinson; government, with Ralph Bunche, in the acceptance of people strictly on the basis of their abilities.

The laity of the church really carried the ball in implementing this decision. The first Negro member was brought by a church officer. The policy was not argued from the pulpit. Rather it flowed from the conception of the meaning of the Christian gospel. The results have not been spectacular statistically. Some twenty Negroes attend church regularly, out of a total of 180 to 200. Seven are members. A dozen white families have left the church, but the rest seem happy to participate in the experiment of having their church minister to all the people in the community.

Even where the Negroes or other minority groups engulf an entire area, valuable preparatory work can be done by a pre-existing white church before the church is turned over to the new group. This was done very smoothly by a church in Brooklyn when Puerto Ricans invaded their neighborhood. For several years Puerto Rican children were welcomed into the church school, and a Spanish-speaking congregation was encouraged to meet on Sunday afternoons. Eventually, the church building and all the assets of the congregation were turned over to the denominational board for the use of the Puerto Rican congregation. This step was taken with good will and in the interests of the Kingdom and was not regarded as an unfortunate solution forced upon the congregation.

Other churches have shown that people of different cultures and disparate national and racial backgrounds can join together in worship and Christian fellowship harmoniously and happily. The poor can worship with the rich, the Mexicans with other Californians, Italians with other New Yorkers, Mayflower descendants with DP's, Negroes with whites. Our Christianity, not to mention our democracy, will be the better for the experience.

4. AN UNDERSTANDING OF LABOR AND ITS PROBLEMS

There is an encouraging recognition on the part of church leaders that the Protestant churches have been too aloof from the life and problems of the industrial worker both in the suburbs and the city. We are finding that an increasing number of laymen are bringing to bear upon the activities of their labor unions the principles of their Christian faith.

John Ramsey, an active church member and a leader in the CIO, out of Christian conviction has made his particular union a genuine force for community betterment. There are many others who, as Christians, are thinking of their unions not simply as protective devices for the workers but as instrumentalities of service to the entire community.

An increasing number of ministers are seeking to understand the problems of labor so as to be able to talk the language of the worker. For example, the Presbyterian Institute of Industrial Relations, a pioneer venture in the field of industrial ministry, trains pastors for service in urban industrial areas through practical laboratory training. Three week seminars for active pastors are held each winter, at McCormick Seminary in Chicago and on the West Coast, for training in labor history and the fundamentals of labor relations. They are held, as Dean Marshal L. Scott puts it, "not to turn ministers into labor relations experts but to make better ministers of them." Through visits to factories, interviews with industrialists and union leaders, and discussion sessions, they learn to gear their ministry to the average urban working man.

A summer Minister-in-Industry program takes around forty-five theological students a year into the mills and factories for a down to earth work experience where, working incognito, they get an idea of what their co-workers are really like. The field work is rounded out with study in evening seminars.

Of the some 750 or more ministers and theological students trained at the Presbyterian Institute, the majority have either gone back to apply what they have learned in their own pastorates or sought out fresh opportunities for a ministry geared to an industrial neighborhood.

As most of the people in the inner city and in the industrial suburbs are unskilled or skilled workers in shops and factories, it is difficult to see how a church ministering to such areas can hope to interest the workers unless the minister and his people can deal with their problems and their aspirations sympathetically and understandingly.

5. A CONCERN FOR SOCIAL RIGHTEOUSNESS

It is difficult to see how any church can labor in the inner city without developing in its members a great concern for the solution of some of the social problems that weigh so heavily upon the residents of such an area.

An important city church with a notable record as a great preaching center requested that a study be made of a deteriorated area adjacent to the avenue on which the church occupied a prominent corner. The study made of conditions contained this observation:

> It is doubtful if a congregation can worship in the midst of a population that has 10 per cent truancy, rats biting children and traffic maiming them, and not experience dry rot unless it becomes concerned about them. It is doubtful if a congregation can, because of social, class, or economic status, wall itself off psychologically from a neighborhood in which it worships and allow man to be set against man by the deleterious, frustrating conditions under which men live, without having its own spiritual life wither. . . . Churches are too often walled off from the main stream of life by their comparative affluence. . . . Can this church bridge the chasm between "its kind of people" and the rest of the neighborhood, so typical of the city and its problems, and in its potentialities?

The church has taken this admonition to heart and is addressing itself to its community responsibility with vigor and vision. There are scores of other churches, similarly situated, that need to have this sort of sermon preached to them.

Very often a concern for the solution of social problems

will bring little return to the church in terms of additional church members. But it will bear witness to the fact that the Protestant churches carry upon their hearts and consciences the burdens of the poor.

People living in slums are often overcome with the feeling of hopelessness. They believe that everyone is against them and that it is useless to try to do anything. Churches can demonstrate their concern. The part played by the Church of the Brethren in the Baltimore plan for slum rehabilitation is a case in point.

The First Church of the Brethren set about to demonstrate that something can be done about slum conditions. The church bought one of the worst houses in a slum area. They formed a nonprofit corporation, Brotherhood Service, Inc., to raise the money for the purchase of the house and its rehabilitation. It took $1,200 to purchase the old dwelling and $1,800 to renovate it.

The remodeling of the house served as a demonstration of sturdy and inexpensive repair work and, when completed, was turned over to the city as a demonstration and information center. A group of volunteers from the church have staffed the referral center, advised owner occupants of the area as to how to proceed with repairs on their own buildings and assisted in the recreational program of one of the nearby churches. This group has been trained to know about housing law enforcement and referrals to social agencies. They have helped with their own physical labor to make repairs for old and infirm tenants. They have created a friendship center. The executive of the Citizens' Planning and Housing Association of Baltimore testifies: "We believe that the existence of this Pilot House will mean that neighborhood people will be much more likely to follow up on needed repairs, since they can do so by reporting their problems at this neighborhood center rather than going to City Hall and getting the run around."

It is doubtful if this Pilot House has brought many new members to the First Church of the Brethren. But it has provided an example of far reaching social service of which every member of that church should be proud. More exhibitions of social concern implemented in such a practical fashion will make the Protestant churches more potent factors in the inner city than they are at present.

Leaders of churches serving minority groups in inner city areas can become valuable interpreters of the groups they serve. There is much misinformation and misunderstanding current concerning the Negroes, the Mexicans, the Puerto Ricans, and other groups. Ministers serving them can see to it that the public receives a fair impression of the group and knows that to think of them as a menace or a "problem" is one-sided and unjust, as they also present a potential and an opportunity.

Steps taken to highlight the cultural assets of such groups constitute a distinct contribution to our national unity.

6. CENTERS OF FRIENDLINESS

One student of the city and its problems quoted a typical inner city resident as saying: "I think there's got to be in every ward somebody that any bloke can come to, no matter what he's done, and get help."

Centers of friendly service—that is what inner city

churches can be. But many of them are closed except for the regular services and have iron gates across the door. Or, if they are open, it is hard to find the way to the minister through all the corridors, past all the doors, up all the stairs and past the guarding secretary or sexton. Most city church buildings look like institutions, and many city churches *are* institutions, with little of the warm and welcoming atmosphere that beckons those in trouble.

The Neighborhood Houses, Homes of Friendly Service, and Christian centers that some church groups have fostered overcome this handicap. In one missionary venture in the inner city the work is carried on in stores, in order to make the minister visible and accessible to every passer-by.

Whatever the equipment or method employed, it is certain that a church in the inner city must be open and welcoming, a center of genuine friendliness to "any bloke" who needs help.

7. FLEXIBILITY

The only thing one can be certain about in the inner city is that conditions are bound to change. One type of population is succeeded by another radically different. Old residences degenerate into slums. Slums are eradicated to make way for housing projects. An area long thought of as lower middle class suddenly becomes fashionable. Superhighways bisect communities and wall off one district from its neighbor. New lines of transportation open up new areas and empty others.

The church as a social institution has a way of becoming rigid and inflexible. People become bound by tradition, im-

114

paled to one spot by sentiment. "We have never done that in this church" is their clinching argument. Such a church might as well sell its property and move out, for it will die a withering death in any event.

But a church can change. People can change it. For example, one church has ministered successively over seventy-five years to Germans, Italians, Russians, Ukrainians, Chinese, Puerto Ricans, and Negroes. Representatives of all these groups are still in the congregation. When changes occurred the only moving that was done was a moving out to meet them. We cannot put a church building on wheels and move it to a better location. But the church program can be put on wheels that will help it to circulate among all the people in a community, no matter how changed the neighborhood may be.

8. A SOUND FINANCIAL BASE

An adequate church program in the inner city is expensive. A church with an $8,500 budget, providing for a minister, a part time secretary, a part time sexton, and a part time organist, cannot meet the needs of the inner city. The church must be open every day. The needs for recreational and educational programs, constant visitation, counseling, and social case work, and participation in community activities require a multiple staff and a budget of from $15,000 to $50,000 a year. There are churches that could utilize their large endowments to advantage in nearby inner city situations instead of beautifying their already beautiful sanctuaries or stepping up their already large budgets for music. And it has been demonstrated that funds can be raised for the support of inner city enterprises if needs are interestingly and dramatically set forth. One project has succeeded in interesting the church people of the city and its suburbs to the tune of $85,000 a year, in the course of five years. Church people like to have a share in meeting stark human need. The Evangelical and Reformed Church is proving that such is the case in St. Louis, the Episcopal Church in Jersey City and New York, the Presbyterian Church, U. S. A., in Chicago, the American Baptist Convention in its Christian centers in various cities. The suburbs may be the areas of high potential if one is thinking of institutional growth. But the inner city is the high potential area if one is thinking of the meeting of human need by the church of Christ.

9. A GROUP MINISTRY

It has become increasingly apparent in recent years that one who ministers to the inner city confronts a difficult and lonely task. Accordingly, the Episcopal Church, in its new emphasis upon the inner city and its problems and in its attempt to revitalize old parishes in terms of community needs, is throwing into such areas teams of workers, often as many as six members of the clergy and additional lay workers. This group ministry aims to recruit in the community Christians who will become militant Christians and who will in turn build around themselves a larger community of the faithful. The clergy and the militant Christians are to find and demonstrate the meaning of Christian fellowship in worship and in service and are to infiltrate the existing parish organizations with their own militant spirit. The East Harlem Protestant Parish in New York City has found in a

116

group ministry of like-minded individuals, committed to service in the inner city, one of its great sources of strength.

In other church centers staff members find in one another and in staff members of similar centers a sense of fellowship that goes far to compensate for the taxing of bodily strength and spiritual reserves inevitably involved in such a ministry. We cannot throw a minister and an associate into those difficult areas and leave them alone to sink or swim. They need the moral support of companionship.

The inner city, then, offers to the Protestant churches their greatest missionary challenge and opportunity. Some churches are addressing themselves to it with courage and vision. But it must be said in all candor that this is Protestantism's most neglected field. Our approaches, with some significant exceptions, have been too timid and too circumscribed. It is high time for the Protestant churches to become imbued with such a great, compelling sense of mission to these areas that they will be led into more programs that are inclusive in scope. They need to deal courageously with social issues, to become more flexible, to have sufficient financial support, and to establish a warm fellowship of those who would prove themselves true friends of Jesus by becoming the friends of the lowliest and the lost.

| THE CHURCH IN THE CITY'S
RESIDENTIAL AREAS

"When it goes well with the
righteous the city rejoices"

INFINITE variety—that is the word for the American city.
Just as one can find in our cities the widest possible variety
of stores, restaurants, nationalities, and races, so one can
find all the various types of churches that the religious life
of America offers. In addition to the Roman Catholic parishes, Jewish synagogues (orthodox, conservative, and reformed), and Eastern Orthodox churches (Russian, Greek,
Serbian, etc.), in our American cities are to be found all
of the 225 varieties of church bodies that our divided
Protestantism provides. City churches range from tiny store
front churches with a dozen members to huge congregations with ten thousand or more members. Their budgets
range from a few hundred dollars to half a million. Some
congregations are made up primarily of poor people, some of
the middle income group, and some of the rich and fashionable, but more of them are a mixture of all classes.

There are churches representing the extremes of theological conservatism and liberalism and every possible intermediate theological position. These theological differences are to be found even within the same denomination.

Then, too, every city is different from every other city, and the character of our city churches will vary accordingly. It makes considerable difference to the program of a local church whether it is located in a small city, under 25,000, a medium sized city, under 100,000, a large city of 100,000 to 500,000, or a metropolis over 500,000. Professor Leiffer has also pointed out the variant types of American cities: the commercial city, the industrial city, and the resort city.[1] In an appendix of his book he cites as examples of the commercial city: Des Moines, Duluth, El Paso, Montgomery, Salt Lake City, and Wichita; of the industrial city: Altoona, Binghamton, Evansville, Scranton, Tacoma, and Winston-Salem; and of the resort city: Atlantic City, Miami, and San Diego. Anyone who knows the differences between these cities will realize that the nature and program of churches located in them will vary materially.

. . .   *The Varied Backgrounds of Cities*

The historical development of a city and its cultural background may have a profound effect upon its religious life, as Professor Leiffer points out.[2] Iowa was settled by white Americans who came from our northeastern states

---

[1] *City and Church in Transition,* by Murray H. Leiffer, pp. 32-33. Chicago, Willett, Clark and Co., 1938.
[2] *Ibid.,* pp. 141 ff.

and by immigrants from the Protestant sections of Europe. As a result, Iowa and Des Moines, its principal city, have been Protestant strongholds. Consequently, a great majority of the church people of Des Moines belong to the Methodist, Presbyterian, and Baptist denominations.

Duluth, on the other hand, serves a territory that was settled chiefly by German and Scandinavian immigrants. As a consequence of this community background, the religious life of Duluth is dominated by the Lutheran and Roman Catholic Churches.

Lancaster, Pennsylvania, is in the center of the "Pennsylvania Dutch" country, its cultural and economic background being colored by the German immigrants who settled in this area in the early eighteenth century. For the most part, these immigrants came from the Rhineland and the Palatinate and were predominantly Protestant. Accordingly, the religious life of this section is dominated by the Lutheran Church, the Reformed branch of the present Evangelical and Reformed Church and, particularly in the surrounding rural areas, by the German sects: the Amish, the Mennonites, the Brethren in Christ (the Dunkards). The Roman Catholic Church constitutes a definite minority, but it, too, is German in its background. The Scotch Irish who arrived later in this area are also well represented by the Presbyterian Church.

El Paso, Texas, with one half of its population Mexican and nominally Roman Catholic, creates an entirely different cultural and religious atmosphere for the program of the Protestant churches, as does Burlington, Vermont, and Lewiston, Maine, with their large minorities of French

Canadians, who are devoted adherents to the Roman Catholic faith.

Southern cities such as Atlanta, Georgia, Montgomery, Alabama, and Memphis, Tennessee, have been little affected by Roman Catholic and Jewish immigration, having relied upon their large Negro populations for labor. Both among the white and the Negro populations of these cities the strong denominations are the Baptist and the Methodist. The cities are well churched, and the churches are attended in such numbers and with such enthusiasm as to draw the envy of many a Northern pastor.

Far different is the situation in New York, where the Protestants are greatly outnumbered by the Roman Catholic and Jewish elements in the population and where the Protestant churches must operate in the midst of a polyglot population of every conceivable faith or lack of it. Chicago, Philadelphia, Detroit, and Los Angeles also present to the Protestant churches the complicated problems of a great metropolis.

Stable Residential Areas

Out of all these varieties of cities and churches let us isolate for special treatment the Protestant churches located in the relatively stable residential areas of our cities. In the small and medium sized cities the people in such areas live in unpretentious but comfortable homes of their own or in small apartment buildings. The larger the city the greater is the proportion of apartment house dwellers and the more pronounced are the differences in economic and social

121

status. But, on the whole, it is in these residential areas, together with the suburbs, to be dealt with in the next chapter, that we find the bulk of the great middle and upper classes of urban America. When we think of the American city, we are apt to envision towering skyscrapers, gigantic factories, spectacular recreational facilities, or the depressing slums of the inner city. But the major portion of city land used for residential purposes is occupied by these relatively stable communities. They constitute the city's most important areas.

. . . *Churches in Residential Areas*

Stable residential areas are the happy hunting grounds for urban churches. Here the Protestant denominations have staked out their claims in a manner that often results in over-churching. It is a common sight to observe three or four Protestant churches clustered together within a few blocks of one another.

The churches in such areas present a wide variety of programs, from one that is simple and traditional to one that is highly developed and imaginative. Generally speaking, however, such churches are traditional, differing little in church architecture, pastoral leadership, and parish program from the small town church. There is a Sunday morning worship service, sometimes a less formal evening service, a church school, a women's organization, and a young people's society, with occasional church dinners and other social gatherings. The average church has a very modest budget, providing for a minister on minimum salary, a part time sexton, and an organist. Its membership will average 250, with a church school considerably smaller.

These are modest institutions, but their influence upon the life of our cities must not be underestimated. The ministries of these churches, through worship, religious education, the development of Christian fellowship, and service to the needy of the world through their missionary programs, are vitally important. By such means religion is handed down from generation to generation. The meeting of human needs in the great crises of life—marriage, birth, adolescence, the choice of vocation, sickness, failure, and death—by a devoted pastor, provides to our cities the substantial, morally sensitive, civically responsible, and spiritually minded citizenry upon which our urban social structure rests.

But such churches have their problems, which are not to be overlooked in any consideration of the missionary task of the church in the city.

. . .   *Too Many and Too Small*

In the first place, too many of these churches are too small in membership and their resources are too meager to do an effective piece of work even in this favorable environment.

A study of the Protestant churches of one of our large cities has given us the following distribution as to size:

Size of Membership	Under 100	100– 299	300– 500	600– 999	1,000 and over	Total
Per Cent of Total No. of Churches	14.9	34.1	30.0	11.9	9.1	100.0

The survey, commenting on these statistics, says:

Some students of the city church have suggested, with reservations, that 600 members is the approximate optimum size for a city church to enable it to maintain a minister, with some specialized assistance, an adequate building, and a well rounded program, without being so large as to destroy the close intimacy of the fellowship. If this is a suitable standard (and it is debatable), at least four fifths of the churches of this city fall below the optimum. At least it is clear that the 40 per cent of the churches with fewer than 300 members are likely to be marginal churches, in the sense that the budget is largely absorbed in maintaining a minister and a church structure, with little if any reserve to build program or staff beyond the conventional minimum of church routine.

The solution to this problem depends, first, upon the development and application of a Protestant strategy for such areas both denominationally and interdenominationally; and second, upon a much more vigorous outreach to the unchurched in the community.

In all too many cities there are several churches of the same denomination in the better residential areas, none of them as significant as they should be. There is much that can be done within our denominational structure in the way of merging churches so as to provide one good sized and effective church in place of two or three small and struggling institutions.

Mergers across denominational lines are more difficult, but even that is possible when the interests of the Kingdom have been made paramount. We have instances of effective mergers between Presbyterian and Congregational churches and between Episcopal and Presbyterian churches. We have at least one church that has official standing in both Baptist and Congregational bodies.

It must be remembered that many of these churches in residential areas were established before the automobile revolutionized transportation in our cities and made many city neighborhoods easily accessible to one another. The plotting of city churches has to be done with reference to the automobile age.

. . . *Parochialism*

Many churches consider that their sole function is to minister to their own people and to maintain their closely knit and pleasant fellowship. As a result, such churches are ingrown and parochial. Their members are not led effectively enough to see the bearing of the Christian faith they profess upon their civic and social responsibility and upon their views about national and world problems. Such churches should be reminded of the fact that missionary work in the city begins right where they are. One of the most vital elements in the program of our denominational boards and our city Councils of Churches is the lifting of the sights of the members of our modest city churches so that they may see the wide horizons of the Christian enterprise.

Some first class missionary work must be done with a church leader who can write about "the normal family parish" as follows:

This normal residential district is an area of small homes with yards. These are the homes of those who have attained a moderate success or whose children need play space. More than any other area of the city this reproduces the atmosphere and the conditions of the small town. As a rule the population is fairly stable, neighborly, and interested in each other. More homogeneous than other parts of the city, the parish will have all the characteristics of a real spiritual home.

Financially these people are fairly comfortably off; they can support a not too big parish plant and they will work hard to do it. The program of the parish is that which we might call normal as we have known it. . . . The religious education program reaches its highest development here. . . . Poverty, crime, and the need for social service is at a minimum. . . . Divorce is relatively low. . . . *This parish presents few problems.* The rector's relation to his parish is that of the head of a fairly congenial family and if he can keep the peace between sometimes warring neighbors, life will go along very smoothly *in this quiet backwater of a great city, scarcely touched by its life or problems.*

How any pastor of any church can think of any part of any city as "a quiet backwater" is beyond comprehension. Such a pastor certainly has more important duties to perform than to serve as a referee over the squabbles in the choir or the Ladies' Aid. If the members of his congregation are not "touched by the life of the city and its problems," the pastor should see to it that they are tagged hard by them. It is this complacent parochial isolationism that makes so many city churches ineffective. All that they do and say has no relevance to the life of the city. They are nice spiritual country clubs.

That such a condition can be corrected has been demonstrated by the Department of Christian Social Relations of the National Council of the Protestant Episcopal Church. In its study of Social Education and Community Action in Episcopal churches it has proved that local parishes can be awakened to a realization of the part they should play in the life of the city, the nation, and the world.

Bear in mind that the reports received were from typical Episcopal churches in our cities, most of them surrounded by home owners living in comfortable circumstances. But a good proportion of the churches reporting indicated that there had been study in the parish of such questions as Marriage and the Family, the United Nations, Interfaith Cooperation, Race and Intercultural Relations, Resettlement of Displaced Persons, Christian Vocation, and Church Unity. Furthermore, many parishes reported that such study had been followed up with action, with reference to such matters as slum clearance, health facilities, race problems, and recreational problems.

But the report of the commission summarizes its findings thus: "Many parishes did something, but not enough. Too many did nothing." Those who did nothing gave a variety of reasons: "We have no acute social relations problems," "Nobody is interested in such questions," "We need to be stirred up," "This parish is too busy trying to marginally support itself; it has little time or interest beyond its own problems."

So the Department of Christian Social Relations has an unfinished task. But at least the Episcopal Church is officially committed to stabbing its local city parishes awake to the problems about them.

The ingrown program of many city churches is reflected not only in their disregard of the problems of the city in which they are situated but in their preoccupation with their own institutional welfare and their already existing congregation. Many a pastor will admit that his program is designed solely with his own members in view. Too little attention is given to the unchurched who may be found in large numbers at the very doors of any church in a residential area.

. . . *An Outreach Vital*

Some churches erect high doctrinal barriers. Others allow their membership to develop an attitude of coldness and indifference to newcomers. Still others allow their message and program to become divorced from the problems of city people so that there is nothing in the program to appeal to the average city man and his family. People want to belong to an organization that has significance and in which they are made to feel welcome. The church must make itself known to the community. Too many city churches are lost in the great city. Situated in the middle of a block on a side street, a church may be almost unknown to the people of the community, and little is done to put it on the map.

One common feature of the great city churches described in *The Christian Century* articles is that they have devised ways and means of making themselves known in the city and of reaching out for new people.

It was not its favorable location nor the dynamic leadership of its pastor that was responsible for the reception of 745 new members into the Mt. Olivet Lutheran Church of Minneapolis in a recent year, according to the study in *The Christian Century*. It was rather the conception of the church as an evangelizing agency and effective organization that brought about such a result. This church subscribes to a weekly bulletin listing all removals in the city. It secures names of prospects from the Federation of Churches, from the denominational transfer department, from the news-papers, from the cards filled out by new attendants at church, and from the members of the church itself. These prospects are called upon by couples from the church who are trained for such work. A large committee is constantly on the alert for new members.

Similarly, in the Bellevue Baptist Church of Memphis, Tennessee, it is reported that the evangelistic emphasis underlies every sermon, every pastoral call, the entire educational program, and even the church's efforts at relief for the needy and recreation for the idle. It is for that reason that in 22 years no less than 14,910 people have been added to the rolls for the church, or an average of 12 a week.

What large churches in favorable communities can do, smaller churches can accomplish in some measure. The tragedy is that too many churches do not even try to reach out for the unchurched. They are too busy keeping their institutions going and solvent and in ministering to the needs of those they already have. This way lies stagnation and death, even in a relatively stable community.

Be Prepared for a Change

But to think of a city community as stable is often a snare and a delusion. If apartments come in, the character of the area can be radically changed, and if the creeping forces of physical and social deterioration come upon it, the church will find itself one day facing a crisis. In any event, every city church should be alerted to and prepared for changes in the character of the community, for change rather than stability is increasingly the characteristic of most urban communities.

. . . *Apartment Dwellers*

The substitution of apartment houses for single family residences as a mode of living, characteristic of our larger cities, brings new problems for the city church. For apartment house dwellers, feeling themselves to be transients, are less disposed to put roots down in the community or in a local church. It is easier for them to remain anonymous, and it is much harder for the church to reach them. There is a doorman to get by or a push button and speaking tube standing guard over their front door.

But even apartment house dwellers can be reached if the church is determined. The mail can be used. Members already living in the apartment house can call on new tenants. A card of invitation can be left in the mail box or on the door knob. And in many instances an interdenominational or interfaith religious canvass can be conducted with the co-operation of the landlords. In some new private large scale housing projects, the neighboring churches have joined forces, secured permission for a religious census, and then turned over the results to individual churches to follow up. This is slow and often discouraging work, but it is productive as many a church will testify. A revealing fact is that canvasses frequently show that families who have lived in several apartments in the same city report: "This is the first time in ten years that anyone from a Protestant church has ever called on us." If we are to win the unchurched, we must go out after them, no matter what the difficulty.

. . .   *Removal of Members*

Another change that many city churches confront is the removal of their members to outlying sections of the city, often (but not always) accompanied by the incursion of a new type of population. Both developments frequently involve a loss of membership and financial resources.

In Fort Wayne, Indiana, the old First Presbyterian Church has instituted a two church plan. A mission project was started in a new residential development to which many of its members were moving. It is conducted as a branch of the mother church, with Sunday services conducted in both buildings at the same time by one ministerial staff. As a result, attendance at the mother church has been maintained at its former level and 235 members recruited for the "branch," soon to become an independent church.

From Evansville, Indiana, and Detroit, Michigan, come similar reports of the success of the plan of having "one church in two locations—partners in a common enterprise."

. . .   *Changes in the Community*

Meeting changes in the community involves a twofold problem: how to hold a moving congregation and how to continue a ministry to the old community, now changed. The second of these problems is the more difficult. The

131

pastor of one church, reporting on his situation, describes in detail how he is planning to retain the membership and resources of the congregation for the denomination and perpetuate the history of an old and influential church. But as to the old community, now becoming rapidly Negro, he simply says that when his congregation shall have been transferred to the new location: "We hope to be able to interest the denomination in our present fine, large, and adequate plant for the purpose of ministering to the needs of this area." But must the ministry to the needs of the area (that is, to the incoming Negroes) be postponed until the last white members have disappeared? Would it not be a significant experience both for the white members and the Negro residents to open this church now to all who live in the community?

The problem of meeting the changes in our city's life is one of the most perplexing and difficult problems of the urban church. It requires wisdom, patience, tact, and a great vision of the function of a local city church. But we have ample evidence that it can be met if there is sufficient determination to make the local church of maximum usefulness to the community.

The tragedy of our city church situation is that too many churches proceed as if the problems outlined in the earlier chapters of this book did not exist. They are unaware of what the materialistic drive to get ahead does to people, unaware of the multitude of strangers in their communities, unaware of the mobility of our city people or unprepared to meet its demand upon the church, unaware of the superficiality of city life and its terrific tensions, and unaware of or insensitive to the social problems of their cities. Carrying on a traditional church program as if they were still in a small town, city church leaders should not be surprised that half the people of the city remain outside the churches, their wistful longings for a spiritual undergirding of their lives unsatisfied.

One of the great tasks of the denominational and inter-denominational organizations responsible for local church work is to see to it that the local churches are well located, well equipped, and geared for a city ministry.

But, in the last analysis, it is the members of the congregation who determine the nature of a church's ministry. They can rest content with a limited program that seems to meet their own religious needs. Or, being sensitive to the needs of the unchurched city people who pass by the church, they can press for a dynamic, outreaching program and back up that pressure by their own personal service. Let no church member forget that "your church will be what you make it."

ten | # THE CHURCH IN
THE SUBURBS

*"And when evening came they
went out of the city"*

THE suburbs constitute for the Protestant churches of America a great challenge and opportunity.

. . .   *Suburban Growth*

First of all, the suburbs are the most rapidly growing areas of our country. Between 1940 and 1950 the suburban population of the United States increased two and one half times the rate of total population gain. The outlying areas of our cities increased 35.5 per cent during that decade as compared with a 13.9 per cent increase in the central cities. The exact number of people living in our suburbs is difficult to ascertain from our census figures, but Hallenbeck's count of 34,905,928 may be taken as substantially correct.[1]

[1] *American Urban Communities*, by Wilbur C. Hallenbeck, pp. 201 ff. New York, Harper and Brothers, 1953. Used by permission.

This growth has been most spectacular in California. In the Los Angeles area no less than 125 new suburban communities have grown up, bringing the total population of that area to the four million mark—an increase of one million people in ten years. No less than 45 urban places in California have increased 100 per cent or more in population since 1940. No other state shows such phenomenal growth, although in Texas 35 urban places doubled their population, in Florida 15, and in Illinois 10. Most of these spectacular increases have taken place in suburban areas.

. . .   *Why People Move to the Suburbs*

The reasons for this pronounced trend to the suburbs are not hard to find. Our city people have been educated to appreciate the value of sunshine, fresh air, and play space. Moving to the suburbs gives one status and satisfies the drive to get ahead. To move out is to move up. The development of transportation facilities by railroad, bus, and express automobile highways has brought outlying communities within easy reach of city workers. Increasing attention has been given of late to the development of accommodations in the suburbs for families of moderate income, so that no longer is suburban life exclusively for the well-to-do.

. . .   *Varieties of Suburbs*

There are many different kinds of suburbs. There are rich suburbs and poor suburbs. There are suburbs with a heavy concentration of the foreign born and with a large Negro population. Others are inhabited almost entirely by old line Americans. There are workers' suburbs and suburbs for their bosses. There are suburbs that grew round old communities, and there are suburbs that were built up from scratch.

. . . *Their Liabilities*

Life in a suburb has certain liabilities. Life is divided between the city where most of the bread winners work and the suburb where their children grow up and where they spend their leisure time. The suburbanites' purses are in the central city, their domestic affections concentrated an hour or two away. The commuter is subject to the temptation to put down no real roots in the community where he lives, thinking of it as a mere roost where he comes at the day's end to go to sleep. On the other hand, in the city, he is desk bound, knows little about the city but the time of arrival and departure of trains and buses and the pathway to a quick lunch, and is delighted to shake the dust of the city into the city dwellers' faces when he boards the 5:15 train or heads his car homeward. Suburbs are apt to be segregated communities with considerable exclusiveness. This leads to sophisticated contentment and snug complacency.

. . . *Their Assets*

But H. Paul Douglass is right in referring to the suburbs as "the hope of the city." Because they are largely composed of like-minded people to whom cooperation should not be difficult and because of their comparative roominess, "the suburbs, despite their limitations, are the most promising aspect of urban civilization. . . . They reflect the unspoiled and youthful aspect of urban civilization . . . where, if at all, happiness and worthy living may be achieved, as well as material well-being." [1]

. . . *Older Residential Suburbs*

Many of our suburbs have grown up around little country towns. Pasadena, California, is an example. As early as 1770 an Indian village was located where Pasadena now stands. But it was not until 1874 that new settlers arrived and gave it its present name. By 1900 there were 9,117 people living there; by 1920, 45,354; by 1940, 81,864 and in 1950, 104,577. Twenty years ago one traveled by trolley to Los Angeles through much open country. Now the whole area has undergone urban development, and the highways and automobiles have brought Pasadena much closer to the life of the metropolis. Pasadena takes pride in its gardens and parks and its spacious homes. Its civic enterprises reflect the cultural interests of the residents. Its school system is famous, its Tournament of Roses a nationally known spectacle. Its climate and beauty make it a haven for retired oldsters.

Madison, New Jersey, was for decades a sleepy country town of farmers and a few workers in neighboring iron mines. The opening of the railroad brought it within striking distance of Newark and New York and made possible its de-

[1] *The Suburban Trend*, by H. Paul Douglass, p. 36. New York, The Century Co., 1925. Used by permission.

velopment as an attractive community for commuters. However, the fact that this was a town before it became a suburb and had a history stretching back to Revolutionary days has left its mark upon the life of the community. It has never become just a bedroom for New York.

The communities along the Main Line out from Philadelphia, the communities surrounding Detroit, such as Birmingham, Allen Park, Royal Oak, Ferndale, Grosse Pointe and St. Clair Shores, the suburbs of Boston, Natick, Needham, Hingham, and the rest, the suburbs of Chicago, Oak Park, Evanston, Lake Forest, and the other smaller communities, have all been experiencing a steady growth. Tucson, Arizona, has seen a growth of 250,000 in the population of its immediate area, while the increase on the edges of such Illinois cities as Peoria, Rockford, Springfield, Decatur, and Champaign-Urbana have been noteworthy. The little town of Rantoul, Illinois, has increased from 2,367 to 6,387 and has in the immediate vicinity the Chanute Air Base where 20,000 men are stationed. Washington, D. C., now has almost 500,000 people living in the adjacent suburbs of Virginia and Maryland.

. . .   *New Communities*

Not only have established towns and older suburbs been inundated by the multitudes flooding out from our central cities, but whole new communities have sprung up in the outlying sections of our larger cities. Acres upon acres of farm land have been taken over and a veritable forest of houses made to grow almost overnight. Levittown on Long

138

Island, Park Forest in the Chicago area, Park Merced near San Francisco, Drexelbrook near Philadelphia, and again Levittown between Philadelphia and Trenton, are examples.

At Levittown on Long Island one looks out over acres and acres of small box-like houses, each with its yard, its television aerial, its automobile out front or in the garage in the rear. This has been described in "The Transients," by William H. Whyte, Jr., as: "the dormitory of the next managerial class." [1] Whyte reports that the new residents are "business bureaucrats, industrial civil servants, technicians of society—the junior executives, research workers, young corporation lawyers, engineers, salesmen. The bond they share is that they are (1) between twenty-five and thirty-five, (2) organization men, and (3) all on the move. . . . It is these unostentatious salaried nomads who will be running our business society twenty years from now. . . . [Meanwhile] America's social structure is going through a shakeup, the full effects of which are yet to be felt."

On a higher economic level are the residents of a development such as Park Forest, thirty miles south of Chicago. In another article in *Fortune*,[2] Whyte describes this community. Twenty-four hundred acres were taken over by the American Community Builders for the express purpose of providing housing accommodations for the middle income bracket whose needs are often overlooked in the city with its emphasis upon low rent housing projects and luxury

[1] *Fortune Magazine*, May, 1953, p. 113. Used by permission.
[2] "The Future, % Park Forest," June, 1953, p. 126. Used by permission.

apartments. Eventually 35,000 people will be living in Park Forest. At the present writing its population is 20,000.

Originally the developers had in mind for this community the young veteran with a wife and a child or two. It soon developed, however, that the typical family applying for residence in Park Forest was that of the junior executives in large organizations, who are constantly being shifted from place to place but who need an abiding place while stationed in Chicago. Accordingly, they built clusters of garden apartments renting for $92 a month and a large number of ranch type houses selling for $11,995. These were planned for the average $6,000 to $7,000 income and the average family size of four.

The residents of this community are highly transient, so that for most Park Forest is but a way station in their careers. Consequently, they are rootless and impermanent citizens. Whyte reports, however, that they find a sort of rootage in one another since all are in the same uncertain status. Neighbors pool their resources; lawn mowers, dishes, kitchen equipment, electrical appliances are held in common. They even have a pool of baby sitters.

The Park Foresters also immerse themselves in the life of the community. No less than 66 adult organizations keep the leisure time occupied. One wife complained that she and her husband were so preoccupied with community organizations that she had to make a date to see her husband one Saturday. Shy newcomers are drawn out and into activities by their more extroverted neighbors. Such experience and training in leadership is encouraged by the large organizations to which most of them belong.

This type of community reminds us of the fact that to a larger degree than we have suspected the future of America is being determined by organization men who are being moved around the country every two or three years in accordance with the policy of top level corporation officials. Their pattern of life would be incomprehensible to those accustomed to living in older and more stable urban communities. These young nomads often speak wistfully of the old home town from which they came, but few of them would go back there even if they could. To this rapidly developing change in American life the church must adjust itself.

. . .   *Industrial Suburbs*

Contrary to the popular impression, not all suburbs are populated by the wealthy, the well-to-do, and the folks of middle income. We have industrial suburbs brought about by the decentralization of industry and the necessity of having accommodations for the workers nearby.

Some of these communities, such as Lynn, Massachusetts, Elizabeth and Paterson, New Jersey, have had a long and gradual development. Some have sprung into being almost overnight in response to the employment opportunities provided by industry. Dearborn, Michigan, was created by the building of the River Rouge plant of the Ford Company; Gary, Indiana, by the location of the huge United States Steel Mills in the sand dunes of northern Illinois; Edgemere, Indiana, by the Bethlehem Steel Company at Sparrows Point.

141

These communities are quite different in character from the residential suburbs. They are more apt to have as residents people of immigrant backgrounds, or Negroes or Mexicans, depending on the locality. The residents are apt to be dependent upon the economic life of one industry and in times of unemployment or prolonged strikes feel the effects immediately and drastically.

The life offered in such communities is superior to that available to industrial workers within the city. Nearly every family has a house to itself, tiny though it may be, with space for a garden. Automobiles are a necessity for commuting to the factory, and television aerials jut up from almost every roof top. The community life is less highly organized and is apt to center about fraternal or national organizations or a church suited to the background and needs of the population. There is far less in the way of community resources than is the case in residential suburbs and consequently a higher incidence of juvenile delinquency and crime. As long as industry demands a corps of workers ready at hand, these communities will continue to grow, although the character of them may change as Negroes, Mexicans, and Puerto Ricans supplant the European immigrants and their children in the unskilled and semiskilled jobs of industry.

. . . *The Suburban Church*

Since in the residential suburb one finds people of predominantly Protestant background, with sufficient means to build a fine church building and to maintain an adequate program, the leading Protestant denominations have a good proportion of their fine church buildings, able ministers, and generous budgets for church support and benevolences in the suburbs. The great city churches are rapidly being overshadowed by the great suburban churches. Every established suburb boasts three or four beautiful church buildings, most of them with a parish house or educational unit designed to meet the social, recreational, and educational needs of the children and young people.

As old suburbs experience a phenomenal growth and large new suburban communities come into being, it is not surprising that our denominational leaders concern themselves with the organization of new churches and the provision of new or enlarged church buildings. They would be remiss in their duty if they did not see to the adequate churching of such rapidly growing communities, and funds expended for such purposes should be regarded as a good investment.

The Congregational Christian Churches cite this evidence of the effectiveness of new congregations and new church buildings started at an opportune time:

Place	Year Founded	Present Member- ship	Present Contribution to Missions
Laguna Beach, California	1943	334	$2,491
Seattle, Washington	1945	575	3,323
Manhasset, Long Island	1941	1,701	8,939
North Shore, Milwaukee	1949	537	1,781
Silver Springs, Indiana	1944	642	4,359

In the face of such evidence it is not surprising that our leading denominations are seeking to raise millions of dollars for new church buildings. In the Los Angeles area the

125 new communities have been assigned to the various denominations for development by a comity agreement. One denomination reports that of the 30 communities assigned to it for development, 18 have congregations that need a new building immediately. They report churches that have made out by meeting in old abandoned houses, in stores, in restaurants or in fire houses, but which must now have appropriate places of worship. This denomination is asking for $7,500,000 to help build 250 to 300 new churches. The opportunities awaiting such new construction are scattered all over the land—in California, in Texas, in Florida, in Illinois, in Minnesota, and around practically every large city in the country.

In the older suburbs, denominations had staked out their claims before the increase in population occurred. But in the new communities the Protestant forces face a virgin field, which puts to the acid test their belief in a united Protestant strategy. The most accepted way of meeting the situation has been to parcel out responsibility to the several denominations. This method has been followed at the Levittown on Long Island and in the new Levittown at Morrisville, Pennsylvania. In Park Forest, Illinois, a different pattern of interdenominational cooperation has developed. In these new communities a church can occupy a large and significant place. It can become the focal point of community activity and interest, the one agency that can help rootless people to find rootage in something that will stay with them no matter how many times they move. It can provide through the medium of a wise pastor a counseling service to young couples perplexed by the problems of adjustment to their rapidly changing life. It can give to the children the foundation for Christian citizenship upon which they can build their lives wherever they may go. The secret in such communities is in fast action by the church in locating and building and making contact with the new families as they stream in.

. . .   *The Program of the Suburban Church*

With all this emphasis upon securing an adequate physical equipment for rapidly expanding communities, the assumption too often made is that with the securing of a new building the problem is solved. But what of the program of the suburban church?

A traditional program of worship and religious education, with activities for men, women, and young people, can be maintained successfully by able ministerial leadership. But how is the church to overcome the sense of self-satisfaction and complacency that makes people look upon the church as little more than a social convenience? "Are the suburbs themselves strong in their influence on American life? Or are they parasite communities whose inhabitants are trying to buy their escape from the hurly-burly of the American social and political struggle at the price of a somewhat costlier standard of living? And are their churches more than chaplaincies to such a parasitic existence?" Such are the searching questions that *The Christian Century* poses in its introduction to the appraisal of one suburban church.[1] In the same article the readers are reminded of some typical

[1] P. 362. March 22, 1950. Used by permission.

suburban church members described by Simeon Stylites: "Polycarp Brown, who came to the morning service once every three months on fine Sundays; Demos Duval, who attended two men's club dinners and even played end man in the minstrel show; Mrs. Boanarges Johnson, who drove her children seven blocks to Sunday school, called for them at 11 A.M., and drove them home again."

Any suburban pastor will recognize these types so characteristic of the sophisticated paganism of many suburbanites. He is conscious, too, of the difficulty of ministering to a procession, of establishing the claims of the church to its share of the leisure time of the people, of developing a genuine interest in the whole community and, more particularly, of creating a sense of responsibility for the problems of the city where most of the people spend a considerable amount of time and earn their livelihood.

And yet this can be done. It is being done. We can take courage when we hear a suburban pastor state his objectives in these terms: "To preach, teach, and live the life of Christ; to get Christianity understood, accepted, and embodied in public life; to build a working sample of Christian brotherhood; to develop a thoughtful loyalty to the church, a social imagination, curiosity, and conscience, a better technique of religious education; to invade and overcome careless paganism in the lives of twentieth century, hurrying people; to relate worship more vitally to the inspiration of the vocations, the community burdens, and family life."

One can take heart, too, when one learns of suburban churches accepting a definite responsibility for Christian work in the inner city, not alone by financial contributions through the denominational benevolence budget, but by accepting an inner city project as its own, acquainting its members with the problems of the city, and leading them to render personal service in the inner city. The resources in money and leadership of many a city church has been drained off to the suburbs. The return to the city and its problems of leadership and money by the suburban churches should be a matter of prime importance, not only to the denominational and interdenominational church leaders, but also to the members of the suburban churches themselves.

. . . *The Church in the Industrial Suburbs*

One notices no rush of the denominations to church the industrial suburbs. These are not "high potential" areas. Rather they are actual or potential missionary liabilities and few church bodies are anxious to add to their list of difficult situations. The Protestant churches in such areas are apt to be modest affairs, just managing to be self-supporting or subsisting by virtue of missionary aid. They are subject to rapid changes due to economic vicissitudes or an alteration in the employment policy of the dominant industry. In many of them the same kind of problem presents itself to the church as in the inner city, only on a smaller and less dramatic scale.

As our suburban communities grow in size and in influence, the strategy of Protestantism must be to look to these areas for leadership and support. In order to develop their

147

strength, it will be necessary to devote as much attention to program as to buildings. A plant, a plan, a purpose, a purse —all these are vital—but a program expressed through consecrated personalities and centering about the Great Personality is the *sine qua non* of a suburban as of an urban church.

eleven | GOD AND THE CHURCH
MEMBER

> *"I heard the voice of the Lord
> saying, 'Whom shall I send
> and who will go for us?'"*

AFTER presenting to a church audience the problems
and opportunities confronting the church in our American
cities, a speaker is often buttonholed by a good church member who with real concern asks, "What can I do?"

It is a fair question, a searching question. For the solution of the problems presented in this book depends not so
much upon denominational boards and agencies and upon
interdenominational Councils of Churches as upon the dedi-
cation, the vision, and the zeal of the church members.
The part that these lay church members play is even more
determining than that of their pastors. A minister of a congregation can and should give leadership to his church, but
the effectiveness of that leadership will again depend upon
the quality of the Christian life of his members and their
ability and willingness to follow him in the effort to make
the church an effective agency for the kingdom of God

in the city. What part, then, can be played by the individual member of a church?

...   *Search Your Own Heart*

Primarily, the church member should ask himself certain searching questions, such as: "What does my church mean to me?" "What do I expect of my church and of my minister?" "What can I contribute to the program of the church?" "Am I a church member of this church chiefly because of the congenial and valuable social connection it provides?" "Am I here in this church primarily because of the pulpit ability of my minister, or can I say 'I am here because I crave a vital religious experience, a firsthand contact with the living God and his Christ and have found it in the worship and fellowship of this congregation?' "

The church member should realize that the sterility and ineffectiveness of many a city church is traceable to the fact that all too few of its members think of their membership in terms of a vital religious experience.

...   *How Does God Speak to Me?*

Even with serious minded, vital Christians the nature of their Christian experience needs to be further probed. How does God make himself real? In the experience of personal and corporate prayer? Certainly. Through the opening to mind and heart of the meaning of the Word of God? Certainly. Through the transport that can come to the soul through an inspiring sermon or a beautiful service of wor-

150

ship? Certainly. Through the ministry of a man of God in one's time of trouble, perplexity, and despair? Very often. But does God speak to the church member of evangelism as he sees the hurrying crowds that unheeding pass the doors of his church? Does God speak to the church member of stewardship as he thinks of the slum residents of his city? Does the church member, like Isaiah, hear God calling "Who will go for me?"

. . .   *How Am I to Answer?*

If he does hear the voice of God calling him to intensified service to his church and to the people of his city, how is he to proceed? How can he further a friendly ministry to the strangers in his city? How can he help his fellow citizens to dig down beneath the surface of life? How can he help the church's ministry to troubled souls? How can he relieve the overburdened souls in his city? How can he shake himself and his comfortable fellow citizens out of complacency?

Having searched and been restored in his own soul, let the church member now study his own church and its ministry. How should the church minister to the city's needs?

. . .   *Study Your Community*

The first step in such an inquiry is to look at the particular community served by the church. What kind of people live there? What are their characteristic needs? How many other Protestant churches are endeavoring to serve them? Are there too many such churches or too few?

151

. . . *Appraise the Ministry of Your Church*

The next step is an appraisal of his own church. Is the church building adequate for an effective ministry to its particular community? If not, what additional facilities are necessary? What resources of finance and leadership does the church possess? What of the minister? What are his strong points? Preaching? Pastoral work? Educational work? Community service? How can he, a church member, be of most help to his minister?

. . . *Tapping Denominational Resources*

In seeking the answer to such questions, the church member will soon realize that his particular church does not stand alone. It is associated with others in a denomination, is a part of a district, a diocese, a presbytery, or conference, comprising churches of that denomination.

If the city is large, the denomination will have a City Society or a Board of Church Extension, one of whose functions it is to plan a strategy for the denomination in that city, decide when and where new churches are to be started, what churches need strengthening and how, when mergers of churches or other radical changes should be made.

The church member will find that some local denominational agencies have had signal success in enlisting the interest of all the churches of the city in the total program of the denomination. The Evangelical and Reformed Church in St. Louis has made each church feel a sense of responsibility for the inner city projects of the denomination. The

Methodist Church in Detroit has initiated a Big Brother Movement among its churches whereby an established and well-to-do church sponsors, aids, and takes a personal interest in a new congregation struggling to get a building or an inner city project combating slum conditions.

The Presbyterian Church in the United States has succeeded in uniting its churches in such cities as Atlanta, Houston, and Dallas behind a forward movement designed to provide new churches for the rapidly developing sections of the city.

The Presbyterian Church, U. S. A., through the Church Extension Board of the Presbytery for Chicago, has organized its program in that city into four parts, with a committee working on each. They are: (1) the inner city with its 14 neighborhood houses and 12 churches, (2) the stabilized residential areas, (3) the suburbs where churches are led to self-support as quickly as possible, and (4) the fringe areas on the outskirts of the city, where a Larger Parish plan has been instituted to meet the needs of the people in these small communities.

The inquiring church member will find that occasionally a large city church with resources of its own will initiate and develop a new city project. An outstanding example of this has been the initiation by Trinity Episcopal Church of New York of a group ministry in the lower East Side, through which an old chapel is being revitalized and a secular settlement taken over and operated as another mission church. In connection with this project, Trinity proposes to build a college of pastoral work in which Episcopal clergymen will be trained in methods of church work in heavily populated urban areas. Twenty students are to be enrolled, one-half of them newly graduated from the seminary and one-half ordained clergymen enrolled for refresher courses. The students will have academic work in the seminary and practical work in the nearby parishes.

In Chicago the local Congregational Board has been fortunate in having received a large endowment that provides it with resources greatly in excess of what would be available from living donors. This trust fund has been wisely administered, with a sufficient emphasis upon a ministry to the inner city and its needs to give evidence that it is being handled with real statesmanship.

An intelligent and zealous church member should know how his particular denomination is organized to meet the problems of his particular city. His pastor can guide him through the sometimes all too intricate maze of denominational machinery and lead him to the place where he should find out whether his particular denomination has an aggressive missionary program and a well thought out plan for a ministry to the people in the inner city, in the residential areas, and in the suburbs.

. . . *The Concern of National Home Mission Boards*

The church member should realize, too, that back of the local organization of his denomination there is a national board of missions that has a deep sense of responsibility for its urban churches.

The work of national city departments has been of a pioneering and promotional nature, and many of the most

154

thoughtful and far seeing ventures in city church work may be attributed to them and to their leaders.

The service rendered by these national agencies has been along the following lines:

(1) They have stimulated interest in and provided information about the city church problem. This they have done, first of all, by arranging conferences of city pastors and local denominational leaders in which the problems of the city have been discussed. For instance, recently, an Urban Training Institute was held under the auspices of the National Council of the Protestant Episcopal Church. Fifty-five men representing 26 dioceses during a five-day period discussed such subjects as, "Patterns of Culture in City Life," "Human Problems and Social Adjustment," and "Exploring New Urban Methods." Such conferences have been instrumental in the awakening of a lively interest in the city church and its problems in many dioceses of that church. Similar conferences are held frequently by most of the major denominations and are extremely valuable.

(2) Many denominations have associated with their city work department a bureau of research and survey, with leaders competent to assemble the facts about a given city and to point out the implications for the churches of that denomination. This method, too, has brought many city church leaders to grips with changing situations within their own communities that affect the work of the church.

(3) These national city work departments have stimulated the initiation of new projects and experimental methods in city church work. The Presbyterian, U. S. A., Board of National Missions was responsible for the founding of

many Christian Neighborhood Houses in the inner city, notably in Chicago. The Lutherans carry forward a program of social casework, settlement work, and an institutional ministry to the inner city. The Methodist Church has organized a vigorous, cooperative effort to plan and support a number of city mission projects, mostly in the inner city areas. The American Baptist Board has promoted Christian centers in areas where newcomers have flooded in. As in an earlier day the larger denominations, stimulated through these home boards, worked among the European immigrant groups, so today they have been responsible for initiating a ministry to the displaced persons and to our Spanish-speaking newcomers.

(4) The city work departments, generally in cooperation with the National Council of Churches, have been quick to respond to emergent needs, such as those presented in the new defense communities.

(5) The national city work departments come to the aid of local church bodies by raising funds to erect buildings in the new communities springing up around the country. One denomination lists the following urban areas where the need for new church buildings must be met: Los Angeles, Chicago, Detroit, Kansas City, Missouri, St. Louis, Tulsa, Washington, D. C., Albuquerque, Phoenix, Tucson, and San Francisco.

(6) Less spectacular, but perhaps even more important, has been the service rendered by these denominational agencies in seeking out, training, and sometimes supervising the personnel needed for effective city church work. They have recognized that special training and specialized abili-

ties are required of ministers and staff members in city churches and Christian centers.

. . . Interdenominational Aspects of City Church Work

It would be unusual indeed if a church member, in seeking to discover what should be his place and that of his church in the missionary task in his city, did not find himself crossing denominational lines. For he cannot proceed in his thinking and planning as if there were no Protestant churches in his community and city save those of his own communion. He will, however, encounter some church groups and leaders who act on exactly that assumption. Unfortunately, our cities abound in pastors who are individualists and in congregations that are isolationist. In some cases, this is attributable to a doctrinal position that sets a church apart from other Protestant bodies. Some church leaders are by temperament uncooperative, and cooperation between uncooperative people is impossible. But more often lack of cooperation across denominational lines and even within a denomination is due to the absorption of the pastor and his people in the task of keeping the local church alive and solvent, if it is small, or in the case of large churches in making elaborate organizational machinery run smoothly.

The church member needs to know what churches of other denominations located in his community are doing and planning. He may need to seek out the help of the local Council of Churches to secure information about his community and the city as a whole and to effect a cooperative approach on the part of the churches to the needs of the

157

community and city. He will find that the Protestant churches are working together with a reasonable degree of cooperation in the churching of new communities. He will discover, for instance, that the phenomenal growth of new communities in the Los Angeles area has been met by the local Federation of Churches' assignment to the cooperating denominations of the responsibility for the development of congregations and the erection of church buildings. He will perceive that there are difficulties with that procedure. For there are Protestant groups who know nothing about comity and care less, and by the time a cooperating denomination comes to occupy the community assigned to it, it often finds the field already occupied by another group. No way has yet been found to assure interdenominational cooperation by those who just do not want to cooperate.

He will find the story of the churches of Park Forest near Chicago illuminating. Here the developing corporation approached Protestant church bodies with a plea for a united interdenominational approach. After protracted negotiations the situation was met in the following manner. Sites were allocated for a Roman Catholic Church, a Jewish Synagogue, and a Christian Scientist Church. The proposal was made that four sites be provided for united Protestant churches. Twenty-two Protestant denominations agreed, after a preliminary canvass revealed that the residents wanted an interdenominational church and not a denominational one. The Protestant Episcopal Church and the Missouri Synod Lutheran Church felt they must have their own churches. But the other groups agreed to cooperate in sustaining the four churches, assigning responsibility for each

158

church to one denomination. The first United Protestant Center is now in operation, it being administered by the Evangelical and Reformed Church on behalf of the participating denominations. This united church now has 850 members with a Sunday school of 1,300. Two services of worship and two sessions of the church school are required to accommodate the congregation. The church has become the center of the leisure time activity of the community and a unifying force among the disparate elements composing the community. This experiment is being carefully watched by denominational leaders.

The church member will find a different pattern in the interdenominational ministry to the great housing projects adjacent to the Brooklyn Navy Yard. Here a site was secured within the bounds of one of the projects for an interdenominational church known as the Church of the Open Door. To date six [1] denominational bodies have joined forces with the undenominational New York City Mission Society and the Brooklyn Division of the Protestant Council to provide funds for the erection of a new building to house this congregation. This will be the first new Protestant church building to be erected within the bounds of a public housing project, and it will stand on its prominent corner as a witness to the fact that Protestants can unite and work together.

This is essentially a missionary concern, for the residents of the projects are in the low income group and it is hardly probable that a self-supported church will be quickly devel-

---

[1] The number will probably increase to seven or more by the time this book is off press.

159

oped. Therefore, most of the funds for the building and half of its budget are provided by the mission boards of the participating agencies. None of these agencies would be able to put $200,000 into a new building and underwrite a budget of $15,000 annually. But all these agencies together, pooling their resources, can see that an effective Protestant ministry is maintained. This project is supervised by an interdenominational board representative of the participating agencies. It is hoped that arrangements may be made to have the church recognized by each participating denomination as if it were fully a denominational church.

But the church member will find that such situations have usually been met by assigning responsibility for a missionary area to one denomination, which will act for all the others. Thus, in Chicago, fourteen denominations have assigned to the Presbyterian Church, U. S. A., responsibility for a ministry to the Altgeld Housing Projects where 8,000 low income Negroes live. A church building is now being erected, the Presbyterian Church helping with the finances but all fourteen denominations sponsoring the congregation.

In Philadelphia five denominations, Methodist, Baptist, Episcopal, Evangelical and Reformed, and Presbyterian, U. S. A., have joined forces to support a united Protestant church and center for work among the Chinese of that city. Previously, the Methodists and Baptists had each maintained a mission for the Chinese with a limited program. Now the joint effort of the five denominations has supplanted two struggling enterprises with one that has a much more vigorous program and a new building to house its expanding work.

The well known East Harlem Protestant Parish in New York, a pioneering effort to reach the people farthest down in that area by means of a ministry carried out by store front churches, has the backing of seven different denominations. The success of this interdenominational enterprise in securing the support of individuals and local churches in New York and its suburbs demonstrates that a ministry to the inner city and its needs, properly dramatized, can find support from Protestants who respond to the appeal of human need.

If the church member talks with others of the laity, he will find them becoming increasingly impatient with a denominationalism that is divisive. They want to see Protestantism move forward aggressively and unitedly. The difficulties in the way of interdenominational cooperation are great, but if our concern for a vital ministry to our cities is great enough the difficulties may be overcome.

. . . Interdenominational Cooperation on National Level

Finally, anyone who persistently endeavors to uncover all the resources available for effective city church work will find his way to the Division of Home Missions of the National Council of Churches and to its Department of Urban Church Work. Here all the denominations concerned with city church work unite to evolve policies and programs. This is the medium through which the denominations have carried on their cooperative ministry to the new defense communities. Even in the World Council of Churches the church member will find a lively interest in the ministry of

161

the church to the city, for it is recognized that the world-wide clash between Christianity and secularism comes to a focus in the cities of the world.

. . ., *Conclusions*

Thus the church member, alert to discover his place in the missionary task in our cities, finds himself examining his own heart and soul, appraising his own church and its ministry, studying his community, discovering how the ministry of his church fits into the plans of his denomination for that city, finding the place he and his church play in a Protestant strategy for the city, and unearthing the resources available on the local and national level of his and all the churches. He will come to the conviction that local churches, denominations, and city Councils of Churches must join forces, pool their resources of wisdom and money, if we are to move forward concertedly as Protestants in our American cities.

He will find that David W. Barry makes sense when he writes in a report:

If ten denominations in St. Louis are to spend over $1,500,-000 in a year, Christian stewardship requires that it be spent as effectively as possible, to revive rather than preserve the dying inner city church, to seek new converts to Christ rather than compete for the already converted, to develop as imaginative and compelling a mission program for the secularized and pagan in our midst as we do in our best missions to the pagans of other lands.

He will find that such a program can be initiated and

162

carried forward if we are deeply enough concerned. He will find that churches are not inevitably the creatures of their environment. He will come to the conviction that the church is here not to be overcome by the world but to overcome the world. It is not in the Protestant tradition to take counsel of our fears and say "We cannot." Rather our souls are to rise and say "By the help of God, we can."

So the inquiring, questing church member is driven back upon himself, upon his own faith, his own concern, his own zeal. And then he finds that he is driven back upon God, for without the strength, wisdom, vision, and love that come alone from him, we can do nothing either in the local church, in the community, or in the city.

twelve | GOD IN THE LIFE OF
THE CITY

> "And I saw the holy city, new
> Jerusalem, coming down out
> of heaven from God . . ."

THROUGHOUT this book there has been considerable emphasis upon the necessity of organization, planning, and strategy on the part of city churches, their leaders, and their people. However, this study should not be concluded without making explicit what has been implicit in all our considerations, namely, our chief concern to make God real to city people and, to that end, to avail ourselves of the resources of strength, vision, and faith that come only from him.

When God wanted to save the world, he did not form an organization nor merely devise a strategy. He sent his Son. The human personality has ever been God's chosen means of saving the world. In any church work there must be a program, a plan, a plant, and a purse. But the work stands or falls by the personalities that are thrown into it and by the way in which the supreme personality of the Christ is reflected in and through those who deem themselves his disciples. The primary task of the church is to bring people both within and without the church face to face with God as he is revealed to us in Christ.

. . . *Evidences of God in City Life*

How and where can we find evidences of God in city life? How can we of the church make him real to city people? It is often said, "God made the country, but man made the city." But is not God at work, too, in the work of man himself, in this apotheosis of twentieth century culture, the American city?

There are two sides to city life. On the one hand, the city stands for all that is evil; it is full of devils, foul and corrupting. On the other hand, the city stands for all that is noble; it is full of the glory of God shining with a clear and brilliant light. We have seen those two aspects of city life throughout history. Every city has been a Babylon, and every city has been a New Jerusalem, and it has always been a question whether the Babylons would extirpate the New Jerusalem or the New Jerusalem bring about the fall of the Babylons. In the past and today the greatest corruption, the greatest vice, the greatest crime, the acme of selfish materialism are to be found in the city. But likewise in the past and today the greatest generosity of time, energy, and money, the greatest unselfish devotion to good causes, and the most aggressive and noblest courage are to be found in our cities. Birmingham, Chicago, Los Angeles, New Orleans, Toledo, Perth Amboy, Worcester, Savannah, and Seattle, and all the rest of our cities, large and small, have aspects that remind us of hell, but they are also full of the glory of God pointing us to heaven. The story of each of our cities is "a tale of two cities," a city of destruction and a city of redemption. In the opening chapters of the Bible we read that the first city was built by a murderer. In its closing pages we find portrayed a glorious city as a fitting type of civilization perfected. In each age and in each city the city of destruction is present and waiting for the time when it will be supplanted by the New Jerusalem.

. . .   *The Beauty of the City*

Not all the mystical experiences involved in finding God in the world without are confined to the country. If we stand in awe as we watch the sunset over lake and forest and hills, we can also thrill as we stand in a city street and see the outlines of towering buildings silhouetted against the glow of the setting sun. If we are overpowered by the majesty of the Grand Canyon, we can also be moved by the shades and colors playing over the canyons of a great city. Who has not been stirred by the sight of New York's skyline as one approaches it at dusk, or by the dramatic appeal of Michigan Boulevard in Chicago, with its juxtaposition of skyscrapers, traffic arteries, parks, and the lake? One has to come into San Francisco Bay by steamer fully to appreciate the beauty of that harbor, encompassed by the city and overarched by one of the world's most beautiful bridges. Go by moonlight and look at the Capitol, the Washington Monument, or the Lincoln Memorial in Washington and the beauty of man's creation takes on the aspect of the divine.

166

Drive, or better still, stroll through some of our great city parks in Minneapolis, Portland, Charleston, New Orleans, or any other city, and you can find all the messages that nature, with its trees and flowers, lakes and stars, can bring us of nature's God.

Fortunately, too, in recent years the long week end gives to the masses of city people the opportunity not only to use their parks but to get out into the real country. An increasing number of city children are finding God in the out-of-doors through week end trips and summer camp experiences. The "Good-by now. Have a nice week end" wish offered at Friday closing time in office, shop, and factory often is fulfilled in trips to the beach, the farm, or week-end cottages, where opportunity is offered to commune with the God of the Open Air.

The city with its specialization in art, music, and literature is rich in the materials for the cultivation of the mystical qualities of the spirit. I sat in a large city church on a Sunday afternoon when a great choir was giving a rendition of one of the deeply religious works of Bach. The church was filled to capacity, and the majority obviously were not "church people." There was no spoken message, just a brief prayer and then the ministry of music. I have rarely ever felt as vividly the presence of God, and I am sure that those about me shared in my mood of reverence and real worship. Such opportunities to find spiritual inspiration through music are offered especially in our cities.

Go to an art gallery and watch the crowds passing quietly, thoughtfully, reverentially from one of the great masterpieces to another, and you will feel that in a very real sense beauty in all its forms is the spiritual making itself known.

Once open to but the privileged few, the ministries of music and art and literature are now available to the great masses of our city people. A visit to one of our great city libraries, concert halls, or art galleries will provide abundant evidence that the common people appreciate the higher things of life even as "the common people heard Him gladly."

. . .   *God Speaks to Us through City People*

But God speaks to us in the city primarily through people. What a variety of media he uses for his message and how infinitely varied are the messages he incarnates in human life!

. . .   *Through Devotees to Good Causes*

Any minister or layman who really becomes concerned with the outreach of the church into the life of the city inevitably becomes involved in numerous committees and organizations. Many find that there is far too much of this organizational machinery and that they could spend every waking hour attending some sort of a committee meeting.

Charles W. Gilkey in *Present Day Dilemmas in Religion* [1] quotes some verses culled from one of our magazines, which, as he says, might easily pass for the diary of many an American woman in one of our cities:

[1] P. 61. Nashville, Cokesbury Press, 1928.

On Monday she lunched with a Housing Committee,
With statistics and stew she was filled;
Then she dashed to a tea on "Crime in Our City"
And dined with a Church Ladies' Guild.

On Tuesday she went to a Babies' Week lunch,
And a tea on "Good Citizenship";
At dinner she talked to the Trade Union bunch,
(There wasn't a date she dared skip).

On Wednesday she managed two annual dinners,
One at noon and the other at night,
On Thursday a luncheon on "Bootlegging Sinners"
And a dinner on "War. Is it Right?"

"World Problems We Face" was her Friday noon date
(A luncheon-address, as you guessed)
And she wielded a fork, while a man from New York
Spoke that evening on "Social Unrest."

On Saturday noon she fell in a swoon
Missed a talk on the youth of our land—
Poor thing, she was through! She never came to,
But died with a spoon in her hand.

While these satirical verses will be appreciated by everyone who has become involved in the multiplicity of meetings and organizations in our urban scene, we must also
be impressed by the number of city people who are giving
of their time, thought, and money to good causes. In one of
our large cities an annual award is made to "the person who
has proven himself a good neighbor to the people of this
city beyond the call of professional duty." What astonished
the award committee when they undertook their first selec-
tion was the number of names that occurred to them imme-

diately as deserving of such an award. With all their impersonality, restlessness, and rush, our cities are full of good neighbors, Good Samaritans, good citizens, good Christians.

. . .   *Self-giving Service*

Here is a man who for twenty years has served as Scoutmaster of a Boy Scout Troop in one of our city churches. He has seldom missed the weekly meeting or a Saturday hike. As the boys have outgrown the troop, their scoutmaster has kept in touch with them. He wrote to them when they were in the service, advised with them about their jobs and even about their marriages. He is in active touch today with over 250 Scouts and former Scouts. Does not God speak through such self giving service? And do you not believe that those boys know it?

And here is a church woman who appears at few meetings and holds no offices, but who, quietly and anonymously, is financing the college education of a dozen youngsters and following her gifts with a continuing personal interest in each student.

And here is a young man who inherited a modest fortune and, instead of keeping control of it for his own uses and for purposes of his own devising, set up a trust fund controlled by others, who are to decide for what phases of Christian work the income shall be used. Giving money without seeking credit for it is certainly evidence of a self giving God at work.

One finds evidences of God in the most unlikely places. A family of six crowded into two rooms takes in another family of four that has been dispossessed. A group of Texas college students, having been convinced by a visiting Negro minister that they cannot square their inherited race prejudice with their Christian conscience, raise $3,000 to furnish books for a struggling college in Liberia.

A Protestant minister in a midwestern city took a job in a local factory in addition to his pastoral duties because he felt that the factory workers as a group were estranged from the church, and he wanted to find out why that was so and what could be done about it. He did not enter the shop as a chaplain; he became just "Don," another new hand. However, when his fellow workers discovered that he was a minister, they opened up to him with all sorts of problems and all sorts of questions.

He discovered that most of the workers did not feel at ease with ministers. They thought the clergy would sit in judgment on them and so they had to "put up a front." But to Don they opened up when he had proved himself one of them. And so he reports: "I never have to say a word about religion. I never have to force the issue. It is all I can do to answer their questions and advise them on their personal and family problems. And I find a surprising number of men who are eager for a working philosophy of life, and for the power and comfort that religion can bring. I don't preach to them. I don't urge them to come to my church. I avoid using the stereotyped language of religion and words like 'sin,' 'salvation' and 'conversion.' But I find that their genuine search can be satisfied and their drifting lives given direction and purpose by the communication of the gospel in terms they understand." Here is evidence that the power of God can be released in the lives of those who are too often counted as godless.

All through this book examples have been cited of God working in and through people. Those who have channeled the city's drive to get ahead into humanitarian and Christian ends instead of toward mere material prosperity; those who have proved themselves friends to strangers in the city or who have found that no man need walk alone in the city; those who have discovered that it is more important to be a child of God than to have all the possessions and comforts a city can offer; those who have learned that with all their moving around they can build their house of life upon an unmoveable Rock; those who have found that the gospel of Christ can dispel anxiety and fear; those who have taken upon themselves the burdens of others and live under the compulsion of a great concern—such men and women touched by the Spirit of God are all about us in our cities.

. . .　　　　　*God Speaks in and through Our Churches*

Anyone who knows our city churches can cite example after example of churches that are performing to a superlative degree the supreme task of making God real to his people. In every one of *The Christian Century* studies of great churches it is pointed out that the true greatness of the church is reflected in the way lives are changed by the power of a living God. In its report on one church, *The Christian Century* states:

Everything that is done here is designed to lead the person to an experience of God, in all his love, mercy, and power, through

Jesus Christ. This is constantly referred to as the "experience of sanctuary." It is cultivated in the personal life of prayer, in family devotions, in all sorts of group fellowships.[1]

This centrality of a vital face to face experience of God in the life of the church immediately strikes fire in church members when it is encountered. One person testified of a church studied in this survey: "Here I find warm vitality, compelling love, faith that really saves." [2]

It is said that under the ministry of Dick Sheppard in London hundreds and thousands of men who had thought of religion as a boring routine of mumbo-jumbo, desiccated and dead, discovered in it new excitement and life. St. Martin's Church drew crowds from the classes and the masses. Into its sanctuary came the cheerful and the desperate; the healthy and the sick; the young and the old. There they found fellowship and privacy, a refuge and a home. In short, it was a Christian church.

On the occasion of the seventy-fifth anniversary of the Broadway Tabernacle in New York, the late Dr. Charles E. Jefferson stated his convictions of what a church should mean in these words:

I see the Tabernacle in the coming years, religious, deeply spiritual, God in-breathed, a preaching and a teaching church, unfolding the oracles of God and smiting evil with a courage that has the edge of the courage of Christ, a radical and aggressive church, making uncompromising war on false ideals and unchristian ideas and the whole accursed hierarchy of the kingdom of might, an evangelistic and missionary church, carrying the

[1] P. 1520, Dec. 20, 1950. Used by permission.
[2] *The Christian Century*, p. 111, January 25, 1950. Used by permission.

world in its eyes and in its heart, admonishing every man, and teaching every man in all wisdom that it may present every man perfect in Christ.

This vision of what a church should be has been fulfilled in countless city churches—in large churches and small, rich churches and poor, in churches on the avenue and churches in the city's worst districts, in suburban churches and downtown churches. What a host of men and women can rise up to testify "I found God in that church."

. . . *A First-hand Religious Experience*

Nevertheless, all too many of our church members have but a secondhand religious experience. "Another kind of conversion is also needed now—decent church members who never doubted Christianity, for years acquiescent about it, respectful toward it, formally believing in it, who suddenly make a great discovery: this means *me* . . . a resource of spiritual power, overcoming fear, renewing courage, directing conscience, dedicating life." [1]

Such people have never realized that Christianity "is more than a great tradition, more than passively accepted belief, more than political loyalty—it is my personal victory that overcometh the world. 'O God,' cried the Psalmist, 'O God, thou art my God!' " [2]

I would make my own the closing appeal made by Dr. Fosdick in the little book just cited:

[1] A *Faith for Tough Times*, by Harry Emerson Fosdick, p. 119. New York, Harper and Brothers, 1952. Used by permission.
[2] *Ibid.*, pp. 119-120. Used by permission.

174

Recall Isaiah hearing a divine voice crying "Whom shall I send, and who will go for us?" and Isaiah said, "Here am I; send me." Do we know what that means? In vital personal religion every man is commissioned with his vocation, called to do something, big or little, for God's sake and man's. The real God is Purpose, hard at work getting something done on earth to redeem our race from its sin and misery. . . ."Here am I; send me," said Isaiah. "I was not disobedient unto the heavenly vision," said Paul. That is first-hand religion.

Ah, Church of Christ, the proclamation of such faith is your task today. . . . If you really believe the Christian gospel—God behind us, his cause committed to us, his power available for us —then proclaim it, live it, implement it, for humanity's hope depends upon it. It is, indeed, a faith for tough times.[1]

And I would add in conclusion that this is a faith for tough situations such as we face in our American cities. This is the victory that overcomes the world and the cities that shape the world.

[1] *Ibid.*, pp. 123-24. Used by permission.

READING LIST

INCLUDED in this list are titles that may be used as reference material. Titles published under the imprint of Friendship Press and still in print are available through denominational bookstores and literature depositories. Opinions expressed in the books are not necessarily those of the author or publishers of *Man and God in the City*.

URBAN SOCIOLOGY

American Urban Communities, by Wilbur C. Hallenbeck. New York, Harper and Bros., 1951. $6.00. A comprehensive and up to date study of urban sociology. Contains a chapter on the organization of religion in our cities.

The American City, by Stuart A. Queen and David B. Carpenter. New York, McGraw-Hill Book Co., 1953. $5.50. An analysis of the social life of the city dweller and a discussion of city planning. Gives due attention to organized religion.

Urban Society, by Noel P. Gist and L. A. Halbert. New York, Crowell-Collier Pub. Co., 1948. $3.75. A standard work on urban sociology. Little attention given to the church, but valuable as background for intelligent urban churchmanship.

THE CITY CHURCH

Church Work in the City, by Frederick A. Shippey. Nashville, Abingdon-Cokesbury Press, 1952. $4.50. Out of his experience in research of the city church field, the author deals with the practical problems of the various aspects of church work in the city.

READING LIST

City and Church in Transition, by Murray H. Leiffer. Chicago, Willett, Clark and Co., 1938. $2.50. A study of the status and problems of the church in the medium sized city.

Great Churches. Chicago, Christian Century Foundation, 1951. 60 cents. A case study by the editors of *The Christian Century* of twelve churches, eight of which are in the city.

The American City and Its Church, by Samuel C. Kincheloe. New York, Friendship Press, 1938. (Available through libraries.) A study of the city as a mission field by one of the most penetrating students of the city and its churches.

The Effective City Church, by Murray H. Leiffer. Nashville, Abingdon-Cokesbury Press, 1949. $2.75. Suggestions as to how the church can build its program to meet the varied problems of city living.

RELATED PUBLICATIONS

Accent on Liberty, edited by Mabel M. Sheibley. New York, Friendship Press, 1952. Cloth $2.00, paper $1.25. A collection of true stories, several of them about problems in urban communities.

Again Pioneers, by Hermann N. Morse. New York, Friendship Press, 1949. 60 cents. A study of the whole home mission task by an outstanding home mission executive.

Call to Christian Action, by D. R. Sharpe. New York, Harper and Bros., 1949. $1.50. While not dealing primarily with the city, the author, long a denominational city executive, is troubled over our urban civilization and minces no words in telling us why he is concerned.

Can Protestantism Win America?, by Charles C. Morrison. New York, Harper and Bros., 1948. $2.50. A study of contemporary Protestantism, its strengths and weaknesses, in the light of the drive for power of Roman Catholicism and secularism.

City Man, by Charles H. Sears. New York, Harper and Bros., 1936. $1.50. Still valuable for its penetrating analysis of what the city does to people.

Crowd Culture, by Bernard Iddings Bell. New York, Harper and Bros., 1952. $2.00. A provocative examination of the American way of life.

Look at the City, by Janette T. Harrington. New York, Friendship Press, 1954. Cloth $2.00, paper $1.00. Photographs and accompanying text present a "look at the city" and show how the churches move into all types of human relationship to meet the many needs of the people.

Mission to America, by Truman B. Douglass. New York, Friendship Press, 1951. Cloth $2.00, paper $1.25. Valuable for background material.

Missions at the Grass Roots, by William P. Shriver. New York, Friendship Press, 1949. (Available through libraries.) One of the pioneers in city church work looks at the whole field of home mission work.

Once There Were Two Churches, by Fred D. Wentzel. New York, Friendship Press, 1950. Cloth $1.75, paper $1.00. A rich source of information, showing how any church can serve its own community, with striking stories about some active city churches.

Take Any Street, by Helen Kromer. New York, Friendship Press, 1954. 50 cents. A one-act play that offers dramatic opportunity for a mixed cast, concerned with the challenge of the church and the specialized needs of city people.

The City Church, a bi-monthly periodical of the Department of the Urban Church of the National Council of Churches, contains illuminating articles on contemporary developments in city church work. Every city church leader should receive *The City Church* regularly. A special club rate to local churches and organizations available. 5 copies to one address $1.50 annually.

The Fulfillment Years in Christian Education—A Program for Older Persons. Division of Christian Education, National Council of Churches, 79 East Adams St., Chicago, Ill. 50 cents.

This Thine House, by Marion Wefer. New York, Friendship Press, Revised Edition, 1954. 50 cents. A one-act play that centers around the conflict aroused by the changes a new minister makes in an old city church.

When—Your Home Is in the City, edited by Lucy M. Eldredge. New York, Friendship Press, 1954. Paper 50 cents. Presents in magazine format a collection of true stories, interpretive articles, and pictures that reveal many facets of city life.

THE AUTHOR

DR. KENNETH D. MILLER has been active in city mission work for forty years. After graduation from Union Theological Seminary (1912) he received a Special Fellowship from the Presbyterian Board of Home Missions to Czechoslovakia (then Bohemia), in preparation for work among Czech immigrants to this country. On his return home (1913) he became director of social and educational activities in the Jan Hus Neighborhood House. Immigration problems today, he believes, are basically the same as they were then.

Dr. Miller has been associated with the Presbyterian Board of National Missions and has served as executive secretary of the Presbytery of Detroit. Since 1939 he has been executive director of the New York City Mission Society, a non-denominational Protestant agency concerned with services to urban areas through community-serving churches and interdenominational enterprises. The society recently undertook a pioneering venture—the building of the first new Protestant church in a public-housing project, the Church of the Open Door in Brooklyn. This church is supported by six denominations; an example, as Dr. Miller observes, "of true Protestant unity in the city life of today."

THE FORMAT

The text of this book is set in Linotype Electra, an original face designed by W. A. Dwiggins. One of the "modern" family of type styles, it is not based upon any traditional model. Because it was drawn to avoid the extreme contrast of thick and thin elements that mark most modern faces, Electra provides a new type-texture for book composition.

The book was composed, printed, and bound by American Book-Stratford Press, New York. The jackets and paper covers were printed by offset lithography by Triggs Color Printing Company, New York. The text paper is S. D. Warren's Number 66 Antique.

Typographic design by Margery W. Smith
Jacket and binding design by Louise E. Jefferson